KU-053-160

Contents

Acknowledgements

 am greatly indebted to my colleagues Rex Pope and Steven King, and to an unnamed referee, for reading early drafts of the script and for suggesting various ways in which it could be improved. Anita Addiman of the Local Studies Section of Lancashire County Library Headquarters has also provided invaluable help by reading and editing the script, whilst her colleague, Judith Swarbrick, has unearthed much of the source material on which it is based. I am grateful, too, for the help given by Alistair Hodge and Bart Cline of Carnegie Publishing and Peter Hargreaves, Managing Director of Hilden Manufacturing Co. Ltd. Finally, I would like to thank my wife Carol for help in numerous ways, especially in checking proofs and compiling the index.

Introduction

his book provides a historical overview of the Lancashire cotton industry. It begins with developments in the latter half of the sixteenth century, when cotton goods may first have been made in the county, and continues through to the present day, when so little cotton manufacturing remains. The main phases in the industry's development are examined, emphasising the remarkable extent to which it grew and the profound impact it had on the way generations of Lancastrians lived and worked.

For the most part, the material used is drawn from secondary rather than primary sources. However, given the vast amount that historians have written about the industry, it is impossible in the space available to present and comment on their findings in any depth. The approach, therefore, is to chart the general development of the industry over the four centuries or so of its existence and to analyse the main changes that occurred. In this way, a framework is provided within which a range of matters that have been of particular concern to historians can be addressed.

The book contains four chapters, each dealing with a distinct stage of the industry's history. The first examines the pre-Industrial Revolution or 'proto-industrial' era, when the manufacture of cotton and linen mixture cloths became a substantial industry, based largely, but not entirely, on outwork production in rural cottages. The second considers major developments that arose during the Industrial Revolution period, especially the switch from cotton-linen mixtures to all-cotton cloths, the growing use of powered machinery in factories, and the early attempts to form trade unions amongst cotton industry workers. In the third chapter, discussion centres on the continued, but slower, growth of the industry and its increasing concentration in urban areas. Other matters which receive comment include changes in the way firms were organised and financed and developments in trade union and employer relationships. The final chapter is concerned with the decline of the industry from World War I, outlining why it occurred, the impact it had and the responses that it brought.

In examining these issues, the book draws together and summarises key findings reported by cotton industry historians. The aim is to make these findings more accessible to a general readership, as well as to point to further research activity that might be usefully undertaken. Even though much attention has already been devoted to the industry's history, and a wide range of concerns has been aired, a great deal more remains to be done, especially at local level.

CHAPTER ONE

The rise of the Lancashire fustian trade

c.1600–c.1770

The origins of fustian weaving

 eferences to the commercial production of textiles in Lancashire go back as far as the thirteenth century. They relate to wool. The earliest mentions a dyer at Ancoats, near Manchester, around mid-century; the others, dating from the 1280s and 1290s, record fulling mills at Colne, Burnley and Manchester.

The size of Lancashire's textile trades before the sixteenth century is unclear. By the early years of Elizabeth's reign, however, wool manufacturing was widespread in eastern parts of the county, merging with that in the West Riding of Yorkshire. It was also taking place further west at Wigan and Preston and to the south at Manchester. Indeed, trade in woollen goods had become especially important at Rochdale, Bolton, Bury, Blackburn and Manchester, since, in each of these places, an Act of 1566 permitted the county aulnager (cloth inspector) to appoint deputies. In the later decades of the century, much of the industry's output went overseas, with sales of 'northern and Manchester cottons' (which, rather confusingly, were woollens) exceeding an impressive 70,000 pieces during the mid-1590s.[1]

By this period, Lancashire's linen industry was also commercially important. Irish yarn imports via Chester and Liverpool were already sizeable in the 1530s, adding to supplies spun from flax grown in the west of the county. There are references to linen making at both Liverpool and Manchester in the early 1540s

3

and, by the end of the century, the industry was widely spread, extending to such places as Burnley, Oldham, Wigan and Preston. However, Manchester probably emerged as the main centre. The emphasis was on coarse and cheap grades of cloth, though less so in the Manchester area, with sales mainly to the home market.[2]

Meanwhile, major developments were taking place in Britain's textile industry. In particular, 'new draperies' were introduced by Flemish refugees who arrived in the eastern and south-eastern counties during the latter half of the sixteenth century. They may not have settled in Lancashire, but their arrival certainly coincided with new types of cloth being woven on Lancashire's looms.[3] These included bays, cloths with a worsted warp and a woollen weft, and smallwares, linens woven as tapes, garters, ribbons and the like. Of far greater significance, however, were fustians, the introduction of which marked the beginning of the Lancashire cotton industry.

Fustians comprised a linen warp and cotton weft, giving a fairly coarse and cheap cloth. In Lancashire, they may have been made by the 1560s, when they were exported from Chester. The earliest known centres are Bolton and Blackburn, but by 1630, production had extended eastwards into the Oldham area. In each of these places, and elsewhere, fustians eventually super-seded the traditional woollen trade. By the end of the century, this had become largely confined to the east of the county, extending from Rochdale and Bury in the south, through Rossendale and north to Burnley and Colne. In the remaining part of the county, the south and west lowlands, linen making prevailed (FIGURE 1). Within this zone was Manchester, where varying amounts of cotton were being incorporated into linen cloths, including smallwares, to give 'cotton-linens'. The distinc-tion contemporaries drew between the two fabrics is unclear, but cotton-linens, which were often woven with coloured striped or checked patterns, may have been the lighter.[4]

Localisation of fustian weaving in Lancashire

Although Flemish immigrants established a fustian industry in Norwich, it appears to have had limited success. This was also the case elsewhere, including York in the 1590s, Suffolk during the 1660s and Spitalfields, London, between 1730 and 1750. The indications are that Lancashire quickly emerged as the country's

FIGURE 1.
Lancashire textile
zones, c.1700. The
boundaries are ap-
proximate.
(Based on the map in
A. P. Wadsworth and
J. de Lacy Mann,
*The Cotton Trade
and Industrial Lanca-
shire, 1600–1780*,
p. 79.)

major centre of fustian production, a petition to Parliament in
1621 noting that, during the twenty years previously, fustians
had been made by 'diverse people in this Kingdome, but chiefly
in the Countie of Lancaster'. Lancashire's pre-eminence in
fustian weaving remained thereafter, though Glasgow did develop a substantial cotton-linen industry.[5]

In explaining this marked localisation, attention has been
drawn to the advantages Lancashire possessed for cotton manufacturing. They include a naturally humid climate, the benefit of
which in processing vegetable as opposed to animal fibres has
not always been appreciated by historians, especially with regard
to fustian production. Note has also been made of the advantage
that was derived from a well-established linen industry in the
locality. This not only provided warp yarns to supplement those
imported from Ireland, but also gave rise to an experienced
labour force of spinners and weavers and an established system
of production and distribution.

In themselves, however, these advantages are insufficient to
account for the localisation of fustian weaving in Lancashire,

5

since there is a need to explain why the industry did not prosper to the same extent elsewhere. In the case of the London fustian industry, decline has been attributed to relatively high labour and raw material costs. Elsewhere, the position is less clear, but the range of natural and acquired advantages available in Lancashire for producing cotton goods may generally have been lacking, except in the Glasgow area.[6]

Organisation of the industry

During the seventeenth and eighteenth centuries, Lancashire families increasingly diversified their income by turning to domestic textile production. At an early stage some derived their income largely from this source, as a 1634 document makes clear. It refers to 'the poorer sort of people' living in rural districts around Preston who, except at harvest time, spun and wove flax all year round.[7] Probably, the women and children produced yarn for the men to weave (PLATE 1). Some families also turned to textile finishing, adding a dyehouse or bleaching field (croft) to their premises. Thus, in the 1720s, several bleachers in Blackburn occupied houses with yarn crofts attached.[8] The degree to which individuals and families switched to textile making varied, much depending on the amount of land they held and other work available to them. There can be little doubt, though, that growing numbers were drawn into fustian weaving, and that many turned from making woollens and linens.

The raw materials needed for domestic textile production were supplied by local merchants. Often styled 'linen drapers' before the eighteenth century, their ranks included such leading Manchester families as the Chethams. They operated from the main towns – by no means was all the trade handled at Manchester – buying linen yarn from merchants in Chester and Liverpool and raw cotton from London merchants. Sometimes, one partner in a Lancashire mercantile firm might be based at London, as with George Chetham in the early 1620s. In other instances, the London merchant might employ an agent in Lancashire. One example was Richard Holt, whose Manchester agent, Thomas Heyricke, sold large amounts of cotton locally during the 1680s. But whatever arrangement operated, the link with London merchants as suppliers of cotton was crucial, though Liverpool merchants were beginning to challenge them by the end of the seventeenth century. The

PLATE 1. Domestic spinning.

The fibres were first carded. This disentangled them giving a roll (carding) of fairly even density. Hand cards were used. A pair can be seen in the foreground of the first illustration.

The cardings were attached to thread already spun and wound onto the spindle. A Jersey or muckle wheel (left) was used. As the spinner turned the wheel, the spindle revolved, twisting the fibres together. At the same time, she drew out (drafted) the fibres to form the thread. This was then wound onto the spindle. The process required two stages, the first producing a lightly twisted thread, called a roving.

Linen thread was spun on a Saxony wheel (right). This was operated by a crank and foot treadle, leaving the spinner's hands free to draft out the fibres. The spinning was achieved by a flyer and bobbin mechanism. This allowed continuous spinning, whilst that using the Jersey wheel was intermittent.

Sources: R. Guest, *A Compendious History of the Cotton Manufacture* (1823, repr. Cass, 1968), plate 3 and A. Ure, *The Cotton Manufacture of Great Britain*, vol. 1 (1861), plate 3.

Lancashire merchants also arranged for cloth to be finished and then marketed. Much of it went to London, but local chapmen (pedlars) supplied by the merchants also sold it at fairs and markets throughout the country.

In the early period of fustian manufacture, the town merchants probably concentrated on supplying raw materials to independent middlemen, who often lived in surrounding country areas. These middlemen acted as putters-out, passing on the raw materials to local domestic producers (FIGURE 2). In some instances, perhaps increasingly, the domestic producers returned the yarn and cloth they made to the middleman, receiving

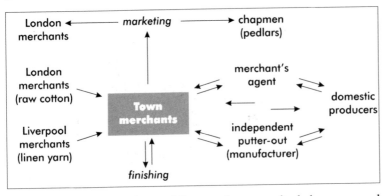

FIGURE 2. Organisation of outwork in 18th-century Lancashire.

payment from him. The middlemen then supplied the yarn and cloth to the merchant, again receiving payment. However, some domestic producers retained a measure of independence, selling their manufactures to any merchant or putter-out. To do so they might attend one of the local cloth markets, that at Bolton becoming especially important for fustians.

By the late 1600s, however, the merchants had become more directly involved in producing fustians, perhaps trying to ensure that they obtained sufficient yarn and cloth of the quality they required. They put out to domestic producers from their town warehouses or employed country agents to distribute and collect for them. Even so, they continued to supply independent putters-out (or manufacturers, as they became known), who became a numerous group. By the 1770s, most Manchester fustian merchants were also manufacturers and they had displaced rivals in other towns. As a result, country manufacturers traded increasingly at Manchester rather than Bolton.[9]

The growth of fustian weaving in Lancashire

In the absence of output figures, the growth of the fustian and cotton-linen industry during the seventeenth and eighteenth centuries can best be gauged from raw cotton import figures. Derived chiefly from customs records, they date from the late 1690s. Those shown in the first graphic of FIGURE 3 give annual average imports per decade.[10] Those in the second graphic show the percentage change in imports per decade.

The figures suggest a sustained but unspectacular growth of the industry throughout the early and middle decades of the eighteenth century. There are indications, too, that the rate of growth

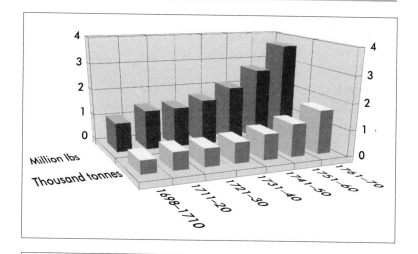

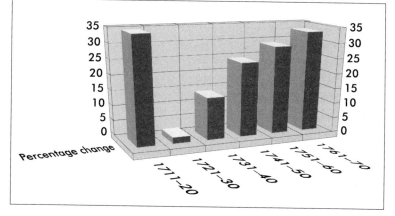

FIGURE 3. Raw cotton imports into Great Britain, 1700–70. Re-exports have been subtracted from the figures.

NOTE: The 1698–1710 figure is an average of twelve years, with the 1705 figure missing, whilst those of 1711–1720 and 1721–30 are each averages of nine years, with the 1712 and 1727 figures missing.

quickened. This is seen in the decennial figures from the 1730s onwards. It is also evident over the longer term. Thus, whereas a century may have elapsed before raw cotton imports reached a level of 1 million lbs (0.45 thousand tonnes) during the late 1600s, it took only a further half century for this amount to double.

One indication of the marked impact that the growing fustian industry could have on local economies can sometimes be obtained from records of male occupations – those of females are seldom given – that appear in parish registers. In Blackburn parish, for instance, of 109 bridegrooms recorded from 1704–7, no fewer than 48 per cent were weavers. That no spinners are recorded amongst them accords with the point that domestic spinning was largely a female occupation.[11] How far they or their families derived income from other sources is unknown. Nonetheless, this type of evidence indicates that, well before the Industrial Revolution, parts of Lancashire were already highly industrialised.[12]

The growth in demand for fustians

In explaining the rise of fustian making, the switch in consumer preference towards new draperies and away from traditional woollens is fundamental. It partly arose from the inherent properties of the new fabrics, which were lighter to wear and easier to wash. Additionally, they offered greater variety in design and price range, sometimes providing remarkably cheap substitutes. Thus, in 1757, Barbara Johnson, a clergyman's daughter from Northamptonshire, paid 5s 6d (27.5p) per yard for fustian cloth to make a riding dress. Had the garment been made from wool broadcloth, it would have cost almost four times as much. Of course, the broadcloth would probably have been harder wearing than the fustian and would have been regarded by traditionalists as the more acceptable cloth for the purpose in hand. Even so, fustian cloth had pronounced advantages over woollens, leading to its substitution for them in a wide variety of uses, not least the clothes of ordinary men and women.[13]

The benefits to the consumer from using the new cotton mixture cloths may in themselves have been sufficient to ensure their commercial success. However, the extent to which any general changes in the British economy also influenced demand for them remains conjectural. Some historians consider that the wages earned by women and children as they became increasingly involved in domestic industry added a significant new dimension to consumer purchasing power. And, with regard to textiles, this was enhanced because it was women within families who made decisions about buying clothing, bedding and soft furnishings. Yet difficulties arise in knowing how far any extra income was actually used to buy home-produced textiles rather than imported ones. This is also the case with regard to any additional demand for textiles that may have arisen from population growth. Another approach, that of comparing changes in the prices of agricultural and industrial goods, is perhaps more revealing. Between the mid-seventeenth and mid-eighteenth centuries there was a slight tendency for agricultural prices to fall more than industrial prices. Accordingly, families had rather more money to spend on industrial goods.[14] Again, though, at least some of this would have been used to buy imports.

Whilst most of Lancashire's fustians and cotton-linens were probably sold domestically, overseas consumers also made purchases. By 1620, considerable quantities of fustians were being sent to the Continent and by the end of the century, outlets were also being found in parts of America, the West Indies and Africa. If figures derived from customs records are reasonably reliable, sales to each of these areas continued to grow during subsequent decades. However, they did not make rapid progress before the 1750s, in part because of the strong competition from expanding fustian industries abroad, especially in France.[15]

In assessing the extent to which demand rose for Lancashire fustians and cotton-linens both at home and abroad, the competition that emerged from all-cotton cloths must be considered. For the most part, these were imported rather than home produced and were shipped into the country by the English East India Company. Founded in 1600, the Company operated from ports on the Indian sub-continent and was soon supplying domestic buyers with a vast assortment of plain and printed cottons. Of varying price and quality, these fabrics could be turned into clothes and furnishings demanded both by the better off and by those of more modest means.[16]

The popularity of Indian cottons posed a severe threat to the British wool industry and led to fears that, because ordinary people could afford to wear attractive fabrics, social distinctions were becoming unacceptably blurred. To protect traditional interests, a powerful lobby of woollen manufacturers and landowners emerged. Its efforts culminated in 1721, when legislation was passed banning the use, wear and sale in Britain of most types of cotton cloths. Fustians, though, were exempted, an indication that, in the face of competition from Indian cottons, they had not achieved a particularly strong market position.[17] However, the ban created new opportunities for Lancashire's fustian manufacturers and, judging by the steady growth in raw cotton imports from the 1720s (FIGURE 3), it was a situation of which they were able to take considerable advantage.

Influences on the supply of fustians

The labour force required by Lancashire's growing cotton industry arose partly through population growth. In the mid-sixteenth century, some 80–90,000 people lived in the county, but numbers rose to about 140–160,000 a century later and to over 650,000 by the time of the first population census in 1801.[18] This growth may well have been influenced by industrial development, greater earnings from which could have encouraged more couples to marry and to have done so at an earlier age. As a result, the birth rate would have risen. And it may also be the case that growing job opportunities in Lancashire's industrialising districts attracted in-migrants. Such links are sometimes evident in proto-industrial areas,[19] though far more research is needed to assess their significance in relation to the Lancashire cotton zone.

Whether the increase in Lancashire's population was sufficient in itself to meet the fustian industry's growing labour needs during this period is debatable, bearing in mind its dependence on hand technology and the competition for labour from other expanding sectors of the county's economy. However, additional industrial labour may have become available in various ways. One was by making fuller use of under-employed, and relatively cheap, agricultural labour, especially that of women and children. This may have occurred chiefly in areas of pastoral farming, which, it is suggested, needed a smaller labour input than arable farming. Additionally, sub-division of land holdings under the pressure of population growth may have created farms that were too small to employ entire families, leaving some members to find alternative work. As yet, evidence presented by historians to support these contentions relates mainly to the woollen districts of East Lancashire.[20]

As long as fustians were made on hand machines, increases in output arose largely through attracting additional workers and using existing fustian producers more intensively. Yet technological advance in the industry, which helped to raise output per person, was by no means absent. Thus, by the mid-seventeenth century, the Dutch or engine loom, which could weave a dozen or more smallware items at once, had spread from London to Manchester. Its impact was considerable, at least 1,500 being found in Manchester parish by 1750.[21] Of more general significance, however, was the fly-shuttle, patented in 1733 by John Kay of Bury. This was wheeled and the weaver could send it to and fro between the warps by pulling a cord (PLATE 2). In weaving wider cloths, the fly-shuttle dispensed with the need to have a person at each side of the loom. Its use greatly improved weavers' output and it was widely adopted in Lancashire from the 1750s.[22] Mention should also be made of the drop box, which was introduced by John Kay's son Robert in 1760. It enabled the quick interchange of shuttles containing different colours of weft.[23]

Technical innovation also occurred in spinning, though its

impact was muted. The main developments were associated with Lewis Paul and John Wyatt. In 1738, Paul patented a powered machine which could spin several threads at once using one or more sets of rollers and, ten years later, he secured a further patent for hand-driven carding machines, one of which used cylinders. The machines were installed in factories outside Lancashire, but neither proved an unqualified success.[24] Yet they did anticipate the techniques successfully exploited a generation later by Richard Arkwright and his associates.

Given the industry's dependence on hand technology, expenditure on machines, equipment and premises (fixed capital) was relatively low. For the most part, finance was needed to meet the cost of raw materials, stocks of finished and semi-finished goods, trade debts, wages and transport (working capital). Such finance was short-term, usually wanted for a few months, and was obtained by suppliers granting credit. This gave time for raw materials to be given out and processed, as well as for finished wares to be sold, before payment was made. Commonly, the means used to give credit was the bill of exchange. Drawn up by the creditor, it was signed by the debtor, who agreed to make payment at the end of the credit period. The bill was returned to the creditor, who could either pass it on to settle his own debts, or sell it for rather less than its value at maturity. This buying or discounting of bills might be carried out by leading firms within the industry. They included Thomas Marsden, a Bolton textile merchant and fustian manufacturer, whose London agent discounted bills on an extensive scale for the trade during the late seventeenth century.[25]

Turning to the question of the industry's raw cotton needs, the earliest supplies came from the Levant (eastern Mediterranean). By the mid-seventeenth century, however, West Indian plantations were also making a contribution and after the first decade of the eighteenth century, they regularly supplied between two-thirds and three-quarters of the total, mostly via Liverpool.[26]

One final point must be made. It concerns the lack of control on Lancashire's fustian makers either from statutory requirements, concerning such matters as apprenticeship regulation, or from

PLATE 2. Kay's fly-shuttle.
Source: J. Lord, *Memoir of John Kay* (Rochdale; Clegg, 1903), facing p. 97.

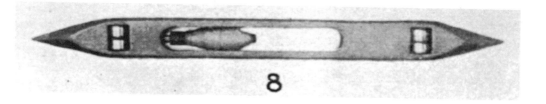

corporate towns, eager to protect their charter privileges. In fact, Lancashire had only four such towns, namely Liverpool, Wigan, Lancaster and Preston.[27] The others, several of which were located in the fustian districts, had no craft guilds and imposed only normal market regulations on outside traders. As a result, trading links with domestic textile producers in surrounding rural districts could be developed without undue hindrance. Moreover, although the corporate towns did try to impose restrictions, they seem to have had little success. In 1634, for example, Preston burgesses complained to the justices that country dealers who had not served apprenticeships were selling cloth, flax and groceries in the town. The justices were not impressed, however, arguing that, if stopped, the traders and their families 'would live very poorly or be cast on the country or go abegging . . .'.[28]

References

1. For details of these early references to wool production in Lancashire, see W. Farrer & J. Brownbill (eds), *A History of the County of Lancaster*, Pt 13 (London, 1920), pp. 376–7; E. Baines, *History of the Cotton Manufacture in Great Britain* (1835, reprinted Frank Cass, 1966), pp. 89–95; and N. Lowe, *The Lancashire Textile Industry in the Sixteenth Century* (Chetham Society, 1972), ch. 1.

2. A. P. Wadsworth and J. de Lacy Mann, *The Cotton Trade and Industrial Lancashire, 1600–1780* (Manchester University Press, 1931), pp. 5–6 & 14; C. B. Phillips & J. H. Smith, *Lancashire & Cheshire from AD 1540* (Longman, 1994), pp. 42–3; Lowe, *Textile Industry*, pp. 44–50; J. Tait, *Lancashire Quarter Sessions Records* (Chetham Society, 1917), pp. 12, 16, 18, 36, 45, 54 & 66.

3. A. P. Wadsworth, 'The Myth of the Flemish Weavers', *Transactions of the Rochdale Literary and Scientific Society*, 21 (1942), pp. 59–60.

4. Early fustian and cotton-linen production is covered in Farrer & Brownbill, *History*, pp. 379–80; Wadsworth & de Lacy Mann, *Cotton Trade*, pp. 14–25 and 113–15; Baines, *Cotton Manufacture*, pp. 95–9; and Lowe, *Textile Industry*, p. 99.

5. Farrer & Brownbill, *History*, p. 380; Wadsworth & de Lacy Mann, *Cotton Trade*, pp. 15, 20 & 171–2.

6. For discussion on the localisation of cotton manufacturing in Lancashire, see Wadsworth & de Lacy Mann, *Cotton Trade*, pp. 170–3; D. Farnie, *The English Cotton Industry and the World Market, 1815–1896* (Clarendon Press, 1979), ch. 2; and J. K. Walton, 'Proto-industrialisation and the First Industrial Revolution: the Case of Lancashire', in P. Hudson (ed.), *Regions and Industries* (Cambridge University Press, 1989), pp. 65–6.

7. Wadsworth & de Lacy Mann, *Cotton Trade*, p. 59.

8. W. A. Abram, *A History of Blackburn* (Blackburn, 1877), p. 203. See also Wadsworth & de Lacy Mann, *Cotton Trade*, pp. 27–8.

9. For further details see Wadsworth & de Lacy Mann, *Cotton Trade*, pp. 29–48, 72–91 & 250–77; Phillips & Smith, *Lancashire* pp. 90–1; Lowe, *Textile Industry*, pp. 99–100; J. K. Walton, *Lancashire: A Social History, 1558–1939* (Manchester University Press, 1987); and D. Bythell, *The Handloom Weavers* (Cambridge University Press, 1969), pp. 28–39.

10. Wadsworth & de Lacy Mann, *Cotton Trade*, p. 170.

11. Lancashire County Record Office, *Blackburn Parish Marriage Registers*, PR 3073/1/4. The figures relate to bridegrooms resident within Blackburn parish. The registers show weavers living in Blackburn itself, as well as in the surrounding country districts.

12. Indeed, some parts of Lancashire had achieved an appreciable degree of industrialisation at least as early as the mid-seventeenth century. This was so, for instance, at Rochdale and Middleton, where nearly a third of bridegrooms listed in the mid-1650s marriage registers were in the textile trades. See Wadsworth & de Lacy Mann, *Cotton Trade*, p. 52.

13. B. Lemire, *Fashion's Favourite: The Cotton Trade and the Consumer in Britain, 1660–1800* (Oxford University Press, 1991), pp. 33 & 38, 86–9 & 112.

14. For discussions of these matters see P. Hudson, *The Industrial Revolution* (Edward Arnold, 1992), pp. 86–90 and Lemire, *Fashion's Favourite*, pp. 52–5.

15. Wadsworth & de Lacy Mann, *Cotton Trade*, pp. 21–3 & 145–8.

16. Lemire, *Fashion's Favourite*, pp. 12–21.

17. Wadsworth & de Lacy Mann, *Cotton Trade*, pp. 116–19; Lemire, *Fashion's Favourite*, pp. 21–42. The fustian exemption was reaffirmed by the so-called Manchester Act of 1736.

18. Walton, *Lancashire*, pp. 24–5 & 76; Phillips & Smith, *Lancashire*, pp. 5–7 & 66–9.

19. For useful summaries, see L. A. Clarkson, *Proto-Industrialization: The First Phase of Industrialization?* (Macmillan, 1985), pp. 39–48 and P. Kriedte, H. Medick & J. Schlumbohm, 'Proto-industrialization revisited: demography, social structure, and modern domestic industry', *Continuity and Change*, 8 (1993), pp. 219–26.

20. For discussion and further references, see Lemire, *Fashion's Favourite*, pp. 51–3; J. Swain, *Industry before the Industrial Revolution* (Chetham Society, 1986), pp. 74–7; Walton, in Hudson, *Regions*, pp. 51–5 & 60–1; G. Timmins, *The Last Shift* (Manchester University Press, 1993), pp. 48–9.

21. Wadsworth & de Lacy Mann, *Cotton Trade*, pp. 98–106 & 284–8. Various improvements were made to the loom, enabling it to weave much finer tapes by the mid-eighteenth century.

22. Wadsworth & de Lacy Mann, *Cotton Trade*, pp. 449–71; W. English, *The Textile Industry* (Longmans, 1969), pp. 27–34.

23. Wadsworth & de Lacy Mann, *Cotton Trade*, p. 462.

24. English, *Textile Industry*, pp. 35–40; Wadsworth & de Lacy Mann, *Cotton Trade*, pp. 419–48; Baines, *Cotton Manufacture*, pp. 119–41.

25. Wadsworth & de Lacy Mann, *Cotton Trade*, pp. 91–6.

26. Wadsworth & de Lacy Mann, *Cotton Trade*, pp. 183–7.

27. J. J. Bagley, *A History of Lancashire* (Phillimore, 1976 edition), pp. 43–5.

28. Wadsworth & de Lacy Mann, *Cotton Trade*, pp. 54–70.

CHAPTER TWO

Developments during the Industrial Revolution era

c.1770–c.1840

The growth of the cotton industry

etween the late eighteenth and mid-nineteenth centuries, the period often referred to as the Industrial Revolution, Britain's cotton textile industry grew remarkably. In the absence of reliable output figures, this growth cannot be measured precisely, though, as in earlier times, some indication is given by figures of retained imports for raw cotton. By 1839–41, these reached an annual average of no less than 452 million lbs (205 thousand tonnes), more than a hundred times the 4.2 million lbs (1.9 thousand tonnes) achieved in 1772–4.[1]

To suggest such a large rise in output may be misleading, however. In part, this is because cottons mainly replaced fustians during this period. Accordingly, to give a fairer comparison, the earlier figure should be roughly doubled to take account of the flax that fustian making required. This results in an output increase of about half that suggested by the raw cotton import figures. Yet such a figure is too low. This is partly because there was a considerable increase in the output of fine cotton goods, including muslins, which required smaller amounts of raw material per unit produced. Also, less raw cotton was wasted as packing and spinning techniques improved.[2] Possibly, therefore, the growth rate suggested by the raw cotton imports was attained, though this is by no means certain.

Further difficulties arise in measuring the rate at which the value of cotton production grew. Probably, though, it did so at a faster rate than the quantity because of the high value added arising from the increased output of fine cottons. At the extreme, perhaps, was the yarn used to weave a length of muslin cloth for Queen Charlotte in 1791. Spun on a mule frame at Manchester, it was valued at £22, whereas the raw cotton from which it was made cost just 7s 6d (35.5p).[3]

The progress made by the industry was especially marked after the Revolutionary and Napoleonic Wars (1792–1815), retained cotton imports having reached an average of no more than 99.7 million lbs (45.2 thousand tonnes) by 1815–17. Disruption to overseas sales during the war years slowed down the rate of expansion, with lower profits being earned and bankruptcies amongst cotton firms rising sharply.[4] Whether, as some historians maintain, the Wars diverted investment away from manufacturing activity, including cotton production, is uncertain.[5] Yet the idea is consistent with figures suggesting that expenditure on cotton factory building was far more rapid in the immediate post-war decades than during the war years.[6]

Finally, the emergence of cotton printing in Lancashire must be noted. Hitherto, this trade had been virtually confined to the London area, with Lancashire fustians frequently being used as the raw material. The trade was probably introduced into the county during the early 1750s by Edward Clayton of Bamber Bridge, near Preston. Others soon followed, at first, presumably, printing fustians. They included the first Robert Peel and his partners, Jonathan Haworth and William Yates, who established their celebrated Brookside Works at Oswaldtwistle, near Blackburn, around 1760.[7] The trade prospered and by the early 1840s, 95 cotton print works were enumerated in Lancashire and the adjoining parts of Cheshire and Derbyshire.[8]

The importance of the cotton industry

The growth of the British cotton industry during the late eighteenth and early nineteenth centuries has been regarded by some historians as being exceptionally important. The most notable advocate of this view is W. W. Rostow. On the basis of the sharp increase in raw cotton imports during the last two decades of the eighteenth century, he suggests that the cotton industry emerged as the 'leading sector' in the British economy. So strong was its impact, indeed, that it played a key role in generating an economic 'take-off', sufficient to launch the country's economy into self-sustained growth.[9]

Critics of Rostow's ideas have argued that the contribution made by the cotton industry to national production was really quite small during the supposed take-off period. Thus, Deane and Habakkuk suggest an upper limit of 5 per cent. Nor, they argue, could the stimulus it gave to other British industries have been large. This was partly because its raw material was imported; it was also because its capital-output ratio was low, indicating that the value added at successive stages of production was very limited. S. D. Chapman, however, suggests that the value added may have been much higher than Rostow's critics maintain, especially at the finishing stages. He also demonstrates convincingly the stimulus that cotton production brought to other branches of the textile industry, especially through the transfer of technology, and to new activities in other sectors of the economy, including building and machine making.[10]

If the impact of the emerging cotton industry on the British economy was far less than Rostow suggests, its importance in promoting Lancashire's economic growth during this period was profound. It is noted in the previous chapter that, by the early 1700s, textile production in some parishes was already employing a high proportion of the labour force. A century later, the proportions could be higher still. Thus, the percentage of bridegroom weavers recorded at Blackburn parish church rose from 48 per cent in 1704–7 to 61 per cent in 1813–17. Moreover, as the cotton industry grew, it became more widely dispersed, insufficient labour being available in the main production areas. As a result, the number of parishes with significant concentrations of textile workers, mainly cotton hand weavers, increased. The baptism registers of Croston township, for example, record only around 6 per cent of fathers as weavers in the mid-1720s, compared with 37 per cent from 1813–17.[11]

Some indication of the demand made by the textile industry on Lancashire's labour force is obtained from FIGURE 4, which is based on male occupational detail given in parish registers. It suggests that, throughout much of the county, hand weavers formed the largest single occupational group during the early nineteenth century and that, in some instances, they were more numerous than workers in all other industries combined.

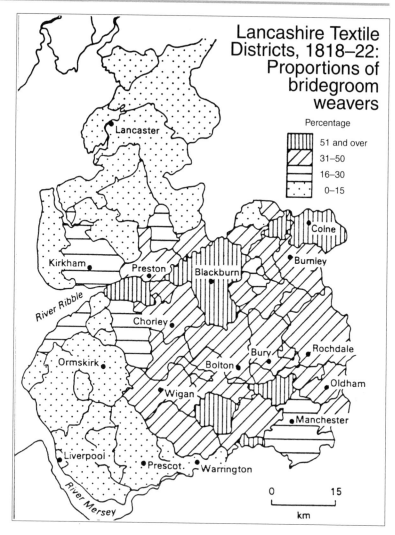

Lancashire Textile Districts, 1818–22: Proportions of bridegroom weavers

Percentage

- 51 and over
- 31–50
- 16–30
- 0–15

FIGURE 4.
Geographical
distribution of hand
weaving, 1818–22.
(Map taken from
G. Timmins, *The
Last Shift*, p. 45.)

Overall, they numbered around 170,000, perhaps as many as
one in four of the Lancashire labour force. Their distinctive
cottages, mostly with cellar or groundfloor loomshops, became
a common landscape feature, adding substantially to the growth
of both rural and urban settlement[12] (PLATES 3a–3e).

The map also reveals a heavy concentration of textile production in eastern and central parts of the county, essentially
the upland pastoral zone. This is consistent with the notion
that under-employment in pastoral districts helped to provide
a labour supply on which textile manufacturing could draw. By
the latter half of the eighteenth century, however, labour supply
in upland Lancashire was largely being generated by rapid
population growth. In addition, the upland zone gradually

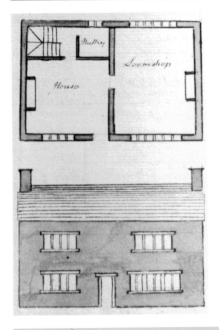

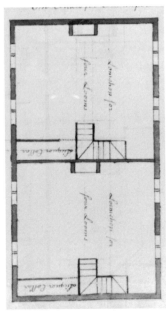

PLATES 3a & 3b. Handloom weavers' cottages.

These drawings of weavers' cottages, which date from the early ninteenth century, were made by James Brandwood of Turton, near Bolton. Groundfloor and cellar loomshops were favoured in cotton weaving because, compared with upper storey loomshops, they made it easier to maintain the humid conditions that the production of cotton goods required (Brandwood drawings by courtesy of Turton Tower Museum).

acquired further advantages for textile production, including an extensive network of canals and turnpike roads.[13] And, as factories began to appear, the upland streams offered a great deal of scope for generating power and water supply needs (FIGURE 5).

Technological advance in cotton manufacturing

By the early nineteenth century, the spinning and finishing sections of the cotton industry were making far less demand on Lancashire's labour force than the weaving branch. The difference can be largely attributed to the varying pace at which each sector adopted powered technology.

In spinning, the development of new machines is associated particularly with that famous trio James Hargreaves, Richard Arkwright and Samuel Crompton. Hargreaves' machine, the jenny, was developed in the mid-1760s. At first it spun no more than sixteen threads simultaneously, but eventually more than 100. It yielded a relatively coarse and weak thread suitable for weft and remained hand-powered (PLATE 4). By contrast, Arkwright's water-frame, patented in 1769, needed a power source and spun a thread strong enough for use as warp (PLATE 5). Accordingly, all-cotton cloths could be more easily produced. Arkwright also patented powered machinery to prepare cotton for spinning, including a carding engine which, with its crank and comb mechanism, provided the first effective means of removing cotton from the carding cylinder (PLATE 6). How far Arkwright was involved in inventing these machines has been

PLATES 3c, d & e. Handloom weavers' cottages.
The two sets of cottages shown opposite (left) were similar to that with the groundfloor loomshop drawn by Brandwood. The cottage with a row of three windows, indicating a former loomshop, is at Top o'th' Lane, Brindle, near Chorley. Several similar examples adjoin it, all of which have been altered. Thus, the garage further down the row was probably the loomshop for the cottage to its left. The cottage with the blocked window is on Bolton Road, Egerton, near Bolton. The superimposed line drawing shows how it would probably have appeared.

The photograph of the former cellar loomshop is in Water Street, Ribchester. It is one of a pair of weavers' cottages erected, according to the datestone, in 1798. In both cottages, the steps may originally have been placed in line with the door, giving a third window opening in each of the cellars.

FIGURE 5. Water-powered textile mills, Cheesden Valley.

The extent to which upland valley sites could be exploited for water power is evident from Lancashire's first edition six inch OS maps, published during the 1840s. This extract shows the concentration of mills and reservoirs in part of the Cheesden Valley, to the east of Ramsbottom.

PLATE 4. A spinning jenny.

A row of spindles is shown at the end of the machine by the window. The spinner turned the wheel to revolve the spindles, whilst, at the same time, pulling out the drawbar. This spun the thread. She then returned the drawbar, winding the thread onto the spindles by means of a thin wire, the faller. This was situated above the spindles and by operating a lever with her left hand, she could lower the faller onto the threads to form a cop. Rovings are shown in the sloping frame.

Source: C. Aspin and S. D. Chapman, *James Hargreaves and the Spinning Jenny* (1964), opposite p. 52.

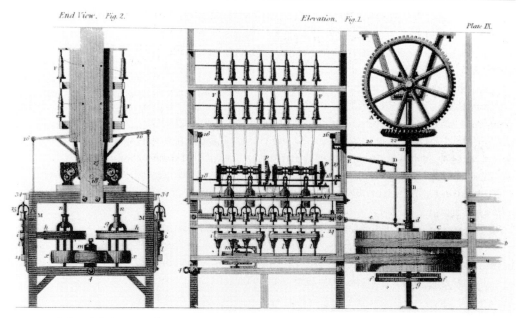

PLATE 5. Arkwright's waterframe.
The rovings, held on bobbins (F) were led through three pairs of rollers (4 & 5), each one revolving faster than the one before. This drew out (drafted) the thread. The revolving spindle and flyer mechanism (15) provided the twist.
Source: *Rees's Cyclopedia* (1972 reprint of 1820 edition), plate 10.

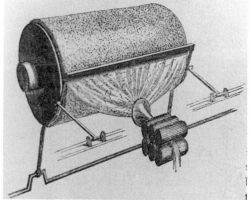

PLATE 6. Early Victorian carding machinery.
The raw cotton, having been cleaned and disentangled, was fed between the carding (great) cylinder and the carding rollers and strips (or flats) placed around its circumference. As the carded cotton emerged at the other end, it was removed by the doffing cylinder and from the latter by the crank and comb mechanism, both of which are shown in the second illustration. It next passed though a funnel and rollers to form a sliver (an unspun thread) and then into a circular can.
Source: *An Illustrated Itinerary of the County of Lancaster* (1842), p. 14.

questioned, but his success in exploiting their commercial potential is undoubted.[14]

The remaining machine, Crompton's mule, drew out (or drafted) the cotton fibres by combining the roller technique adopted by Arkwright with a modified version of the drafting carriage favoured by Hargreaves (PLATE 7). Fine, strong threads resulted, enabling muslins as well as calicoes to be woven. Power was applied to the outward journey of the drafting carriage from the early 1790s, but its return (putting-up), which involved winding the spun yarn evenly onto the spindles to form cops, still remained a hand process requiring a high degree of skill from the spinner.[15]

The demand for mule threads soon outstripped that for jenny and water-frame threads. In 1811, a survey undertaken by Samuel Crompton stated that some 4.2 million mule spindles were in use, compared with only around 310,000 water-frames and about 156,000 jennies. Understandably, Crompton wished to stress the importance of his own invention and he certainly helped his cause by counting only the jennies and water-frames that were installed in mule-spinning mills. Yet there is no doubt that the mule soon became the predominant spinning machine.[16] Its pre-eminence was further reinforced, when, in 1825 and 1830, Richard Roberts took out patents for a self-actor version, which, almost automatically, could return the carriage and wind the cop. However, the hand-assisted (or hand) mule long retained its advantage in spinning fine threads. This was because it could be operated with greater sensitivity, thus causing fewer thread breakages.[17]

Meanwhile, technological advance also arose in other branches of the cotton industry, though at a far slower pace in weaving. As early as the 1780s, Edmund Cartwright invented a powerloom, but it was little used. Far more popular were the improved looms introduced by William Horrocks (1803) and Sharp and Roberts (1822) (PLATE 8). By the mid-1830s, around 62,000 powerlooms had been installed in Lancashire factories, requiring some 30,000 weavers. Yet hand weaver numbers in the county probably remained undiminished, so that the triumph of the powerloom was by no means complete.[18] To some extent, they were helped by William Radcliffe's dandy loom, patented in 1802, which featured a device for winding the cloth onto the beam as it was woven. It was used in conjunction with a machine for sizing the warps before they were put in the loom. Freed from having to take-up the cloth and dress the warps, the dandy loom weaver could work far faster than other hand weavers.[19]

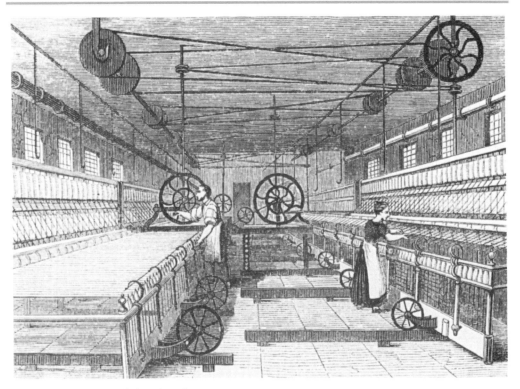

PLATE 7. Spinning with hand mules.
The spindles on the mule were placed at the front of the carriage. The frame on the left has been drawn out with the aid of steam power. It is about to be returned (put up) by the spinner, using a faller wire to produce the cops. The spinner revolves the spindles by turning the wheel to his right. Also shown is a woman piecer joining broken threads.
Source: *An Illustrated Itinerary of the County of Lancaster* (1842), p. 20.

PLATE 8. Powerloom weaving, *c*.1840.
The looms were driven by belt drives. Each weaver appears to be managing only one loom, an indication that thread breakages were still a major problem in power weaving.
Source: *An Illustrated Itinerary of the County of Lancaster* (1842), p. 29.

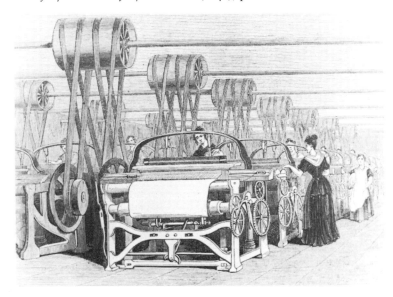

In the finishing trades, power was applied to various types of machinery used in bleach works. This included dash wheels and squeezers, which washed and removed water from cloth, a process known as calendering. Additionally, powered machines became available for printing cloth by means of engraved copper cylinders. These were developed in the mid-1780s by Thomas Bell at the works of Livesey, Hargreaves & Co., Walton-le-Dale, near Preston and soon became widely adopted.[20] Even so, they did not entirely supersede hand printing, 8,324 block-printing tables still being found in the Lancashire area as late as 1842[21] (PLATE 9).

The development of factory production

During the later decades of the eighteenth century, the preparatory and spinning branches of the cotton industry were largely transferred from domestic premises (outwork production) into workshops and factories (centralised production). So, too, were the finishing processes, though the extent to which they were ever domestic trades is unclear. In contrast, the weaving branch lagged behind, domestic work remaining dominant well into the nineteenth century.

Many early cotton factories were converted from corn mills, farm buildings and domestic premises and were often located

PLATE 9a. Hand printing.
The wooden block used in hand printing had a pattern cut in relief and metal pins fitted at each corner. The printer placed it on the cloth and struck it with an iron mallet to impart the pattern. Colour was applied to the block by placing in a wooden sieve, the surface of which was brushed with colour by the printer's assistant or tierer. The printer positioned the block on the cloth with the aid of the pins.
Source: British Parliamentary Papers, *Children's Employment Commission: Second Report*, Part I (1842) p. B7.

PLATE 9b. Machine printing.
In machine printing, an engraved cylinder was placed horizontally with another cylinder above it. The base of the lower cylinder took up colour from a trough, the excess being scraped off by a closely-fitting steel blade known as a doctor. The cloth was printed as it passed between the cylinders. Source: *An Illustrated Itinerary of the county of Lancaster* (1842), p. 62.

in upland country areas, where water power could be best exploited. They were frequently plain, functional structures of local stone. Those that were purpose built would usually be fairly small, perhaps 25–30 feet (7.6–9.1 metres) wide by 60–80 feet (18.3–24.4 metres) long and three or four storeys high. The weight of the building would be taken largely by the outer walls, which, in consequence, were thick and contained relatively small window openings (PLATE 10). Inside, wooden beams ran from front to back, on which were laid wooden joists and floorboards. In the wider mills, one or more rows of cast-iron columns might be incorporated to take some of the load. Restricted sites could limit the size of these mills, though the power that could be generated on the site was a more telling factor.[22]

In towns, where the industry became increasingly located, steam engines normally provided the power source from the 1780s, so much larger mills could be built (PLATE 11). However, they were not particularly common, a reflection of the limited scale on which most of Lancashire's cotton firms operated. At Manchester, for example, 90 factory-based cotton firms were to be found in 1815, of which 71 (79 per cent) employed 150 people or fewer.[23] By 1841, the figure for Lancashire as a whole was around 746 firms out of 1,241 (60 per cent), though firms with more than 150 employees dominated the industry in terms of labour, power and capital employed. Various reasons have been offered to explain this preponderance of small and medium-sized firms, including the ready availability of credit, the emergence of specialist markets for cotton products and the difficulties and costs of marketing.[24]

The rise of factory production was closely associated with the development of powered machinery, though the link is not entirely clear-cut. This is partly because outwork might continue in an industry, as in textile weaving, long after powered machinery became available. The issue is discussed in the following chapter. It is also because centralised production occurred in some industries, such as textile printing, before powered machinery was introduced. Clearly, there were other reasons for turning from outwork to factory production, including savings in transport costs, closer supervision of workers and reduction in embezzlement of raw materials.[25] Additionally, the level of fixed costs might prove too high for domestic producers, as in the finishing trades, where an adequate water supply and space for bleaching crofts had to be provided.

PLATE 10. Early water-powered textile mills. Except for reservoirs and water courses, relatively few water powered mill remains are still to be found in Lancashire. However, some idea of their appearance can be obtained from this photograph of Cheesden Lumb Mill (see FIGURE 5). Built in the late eighteenth century for fulling wool, it was converted to cotton spinning during the 1850s.

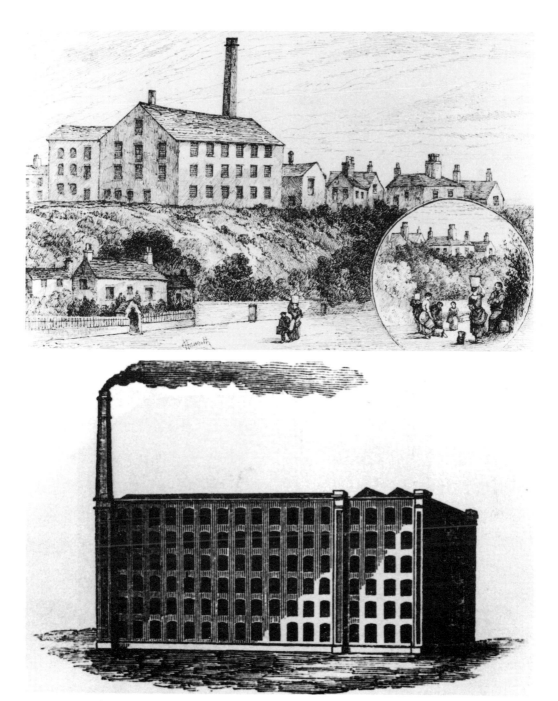

PLATE 11. Early steam-powered mills.

As in rural districts, early textile mills in towns tended to lack architectural detail. This is evident in Charles Howarth's sketch of Spring Hill Mill, Blackburn, which was built in 1797. According to James Nasmith, this began to change when, from the late 1820s, he introduced mills of improved appearance. The changes were slight, consisting mainly of pilasters (built in columns) at the corners and a cornice around the top of the walls. See J. Nasmith, *Recent Cotton Mill Construction and Engineering* (1894), pp. 113–14.

Influences on the growth of cotton manufacturing: supply aspects

The introduction of improved machinery had a marked effect on the growth of the cotton industry through the massive increases it brought in productivity. According to one estimate, an eighteenth-century hand spinner using a wheel with a single spindle would have taken some 50,000 hours to process 100 lbs (45.3 kilograms) of cotton, though this may well be an exaggeration. Early mules, however, reduced the time to some 2,000 hours, the water-frame to a few hundred and a mid-1820s mule to as little as 135.[26]

Impressive savings were also claimed for powered machinery used in finishing and weaving. With regard to the former, an estimate made in 1851 maintained that a powered printing machine operated by a man and a boy could produce as much calico per hour, printed in four colours, as could 200 operatives using traditional block prints. As to the latter, it was claimed in the mid-1830s that, for a given grade of cloth, a steam weaver assisted by a girl could produce eighteen to twenty pieces per week, compared with only two pieces that a 'very good' hand weaver could achieve.[27]

Nor should it be overlooked that dramatic reductions were achieved in the time taken to bleach cloth. Traditionally, this had been undertaken by repeatedly immersing cloth in sour milk and laying it out in fields to expose it to the sun. The process could take seven or eight months. However, from the mid-eighteenth century, the replacement of sour milk by sulphuric acid roughly halved the time taken and at the end of the century, the use of bleaching powder reduced this to little over a day.[28]

In providing such figures, contemporary writers were only too eager to stress the enormous benefits that machinery could bring. Accordingly, in seeking to impress their readers, they probably overstated their case, or made reference to the most advanced machines available, from which, at the time, very few firms benefited.

The increasing use of improved machinery, along with a rapidly-growing population, helped to free the industry from long-term labour shortages. So, too, did the tendency for full- and part-time agricultural workers to become specialist textile producers. As in earlier times, considerable use was made of child and female labour and since many first-generation cotton factories were located in country areas, where population was sparse, pauper children were commonly employed. Their tranfer into industrial work had long been encouraged by poor law authorities and charitable institutions, both within and beyond Lancashire. In common with women's labour, that of children could prove highly attractive to employers because of its relative cheapness and adaptability. And in mule-spinning factories, responsibility for recruiting, supervising and paying children as piecers – who joined together broken threads during spinning – could be passed to the spinners themselves.[29]

The extent to which such labour was used in cotton production must not be exaggerated, however. With regard to Lancashire children aged 5–9, the 1851 census suggests that only 2.8 per cent of boys and 1.6 per cent of girls were in full-time, paid employment. Even for those aged 10–14, the figure was no more than 44 per cent for boys and 34 per cent for girls.[30] The data may under-record somewhat, but they probably reflect the difficulty of supervising young children at work, which, along with their limited strength and powers of concentration, reduced their value to employers. Besides, school attendance was becoming more widespread by mid-century, whilst the 1833 Factory Act required that children employed in textile mills should be at least 9 years old and that those under 14 should work no more than 48 hours a week. This legislation helped to meet the concern amongst some contemporaries about the exploitation of child labour[31] and set up a factory inspectorate with powers to bring prosecutions against employers deemed guilty of it. How effective the inspectors proved is debatable, though they appear to have been extremely vigilant with regard to child-related offences during the mid-1840s, after the 1844 Factory Act gave further protection to young persons by cutting the working day of under-13s to 6½ hours, but lowering the minimum age of work to eight.[32]

Limitations on female employment also had a legal dimension, the 1844 Factory Act restricting daily working hours to twelve.[33] However, a more powerful constraint was exerted by motherhood. At Preston, for example, only around a quarter of married women with children were recorded as having paid employment in 1851 and fewer than 15 per cent worked away from home for most of the day.[34] Such figures disregard an indeterminate amount of part-time work undertaken by mothers, but they reflect the widely-held contemporary view that a married woman's role was that of homemaker rather than paid worker.[35]

The growing use of powered technology and the erection of purpose-built mills added appreciably to the industry's fixed capital expenditure, especially after the Napoleonic Wars. For the more successful firms, retained profits provided at least part of the finance that was needed. But a range of other sources could also be tapped. They included loans from local business-men and merchants, often as mortgages on mill premises, and investments made by partners. New entrants to the industry might find other sources, perhaps raising small loans from rela-tives and friends, or renting the facilities they required. As to working capital, credit offered by suppliers remained important, with the bill of exchange as the medium. Lancashire's emerging banking system belatedly offered short-term loan and overdraft facilities also and, in addition to merchants and manufacturers, provided another means by which bills of exchange could be discounted.[36]

Augmentation of financial services was accompanied by developments in merchanting. Helped by its location within the country's main centre of cotton manufacturing, Manchester began to rival London, albeit temporarily, as the international market for cotton cloth and yarn sales, warehousing functions coming to dominate its economic activity. Indeed, by 1815, the central area of the town had become packed with small ware-houses, the rateable value of which comprised nearly half that for the town's total property.[37] Meanwhile, in the 1790s, Liver-pool superseded London as the principal port for raw cotton imports, building extensive docks and warehouses (PLATE 12), developing an extensive brokerage system to deal with the mas-sive imports of raw cotton and attracting merchants from Man-chester who had hitherto dominated the trade. Liverpool's emergence as the main cotton broking centre was aided by the rise of America as the largest supplier of raw cotton.[38]

The growing tendency for Lancashire's cotton and linen mer-chants to become involved with the production of fustians and, by the late eighteenth century, cotton cloths, was accompanied by leading cotton producers (including finishers) diversifying into merchanting. They became particularly involved with United States trade. This offered the prospect of high profits, but led many of them to ruin as sales plummeted during the post-Napoleonic era, leaving London wholesalers to seize the initiative.[39]

PLATE 12. Liverpool cotton warehouses, built 1802.
This impressive range of six-storeyed warehouses gives some indication of the vast quantities of the raw cotton then being handled at Liverpool. Known as Goree Buildings, they faced St George's Dock.
Source: *An Illustrated Itinerary of the County of Lancaster* (1842), p. 105.

Influences on the growth of cotton manufacturing: demand aspects

During the late eighteenth century, the home market for cotton goods was probably more important than the overseas market. Thereafter, exports seem to have grown more rapidly than home sales, so that, up to the early Victorian era, they accounted for about half the value of total output. Home sales fluctuated less than exports, though, bringing a welcome measure of stability in the trade.[40]

In the home market, all-cotton cloths at first sold largely to working and middle-class groups, but, from the 1790s, they were increasingly preferred by upper-class consumers as well. The growing popularity of cottons reflected the ease with which they could be washed, dried and ironed and the comfort they offered to wearers, not least as underclothing. But, for the bulk of consumers, price was probably a more telling consideration, one estimate suggesting that a piece of cotton cloth priced at £4 in the 1780s would have sold for as little as 5s (25p) by the 1850s.[41] Of course, not all cottons would have fallen so much in price, especially the finer muslins and fancy printed wares. Such products were aimed at wealthy, fashion-conscious consumers and might well rival Indian imports in quality as well as price.[42]

In overseas markets, sales grew rapidly, outlets being found for a wide range of cotton yarns and cloths. Around the turn of the century, cottons had already replaced woollens as the leading British export, assuming a level quite out of proportion to their share in national output. By the end of the Napoleonic Wars, they comprised as much as 40 per cent of British exports by value and approached 50 per cent for much of the 1820s and 1830s.[43]

As to the destination of overseas sales, Europe and America, including the West Indies, assumed early prominence, accounting for around 90 per cent of the total between the 1780s and 1820s. These markets continued to expand thereafter, but took a smaller proportion of the whole. This was most marked as far as Europe was concerned, a reflection of the impact made by the growth of domestic cotton industries. In response, British manufacturers were forced to turn increasingly to more distant markets and by mid-century, Asia, mainly India, was taking around a quarter of British cotton exports by value[44] (FIGURE 6).

Cotton masters and their employees

Studies made by several historians have refuted the idea that Lancashire's early factory owners tended to come from humble origins. As a rule, they were men of substance, often having

FIGURE 6 (below and opposite). Changes in overseas markets for British cotton goods, 1780–1896 (the figures are percentage shares by value).

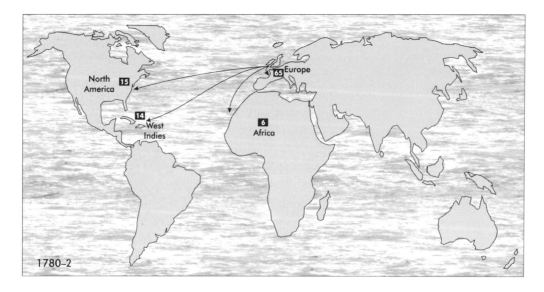

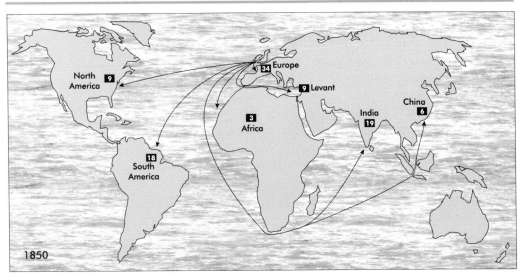

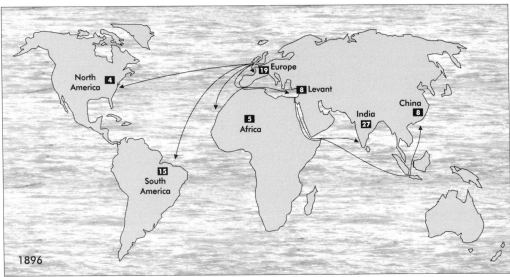

established themselves as successful businessmen within the textile industry. Thus, of the 92 who are known to have owned Arkwright-type mills in Lancashire during 1787, nearly half had been textile manufacturers, sometimes in combination with finishing or merchanting activities[45] (FIGURE 7). A larger sample of 351 Lancashire cotton masters operating during the middle decades of the nineteenth century reveals similar tendencies. The origins of 21 per cent of this group are unknown, but, of the remainder, the vast majority came from middle-class backgrounds. By this stage hereditary millowners had become important and they comprised 55 per cent of the total.[46]

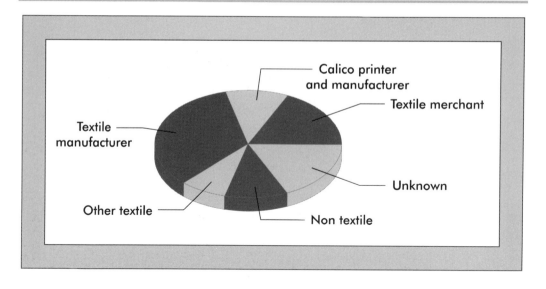

The sample also indicates that, contrary to views that are sometimes expounded, Nonconformists may not have been significantly better represented amongst Lancashire's millowners than Anglicans. It suggests, too, that millowners were by no means characterised by the frugality of their lifestyles. Thus, only 3 per cent managed without at least one resident servant and the majority had three or more.[47] But it is important to remember that success in the textile industry was neither assured nor, once attained, certain to last, a high rate of mortality amongst firms being only too evident. Even large and apparently secure firms could meet with disaster, as in the case of Livesey, Hargreaves & Co., calico printers of Mosney Works, near Preston, and Henry Sudell, calico manufacturer of Mellor, near Blackburn (PLATE 13). The former concern became bankrupt in 1788, with reputed debts of £1.5 million.[48] The latter, thought to be a millionaire, ceased trading in 1827, having made substantial losses on merchanting activity in America and Germany.[49]

A further characteristic of Lancashire's early millowners that has provoked comment concerns the extent to which they ran their enterprises on paternalistic lines. The notion of paternalism has been particularly associated with employers who established factory villages, where they frequently built high-quality housing and other facilities for their employees. However, paternalist employers were also to be found in towns, where they might again provide houses, along with schools, reading rooms, libraries and the like for their employees' use (FIGURE 8). And

FIGURE 7. Occupational backgrounds of factory owners in Lancashire, 1797.

PLATE 13a. Woodfold Hall, Mellor, near Blackburn.
Built by Henry Sudell during the 1790s, Woodfold Hall was a classical-style building of two storeys. Ashlar faced, it had a nine-bay frontage and a projecting portico supported by four columns. (Photograph courtesy of Blackburn Local Studies Library.)

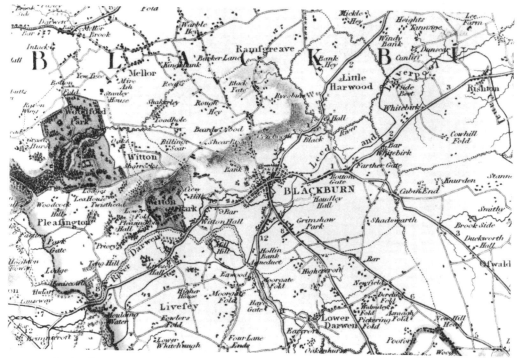

PLATE 13b. As the extract from Greenwood's 1818 map shows, Woodfold Hall was distant enough from the town to give seclusion, but not so far away as to cause undue inconvenience.

their paternalistic activity could spread to various forms of 'treating', such as day excursions or parties to celebrate the weddings of their children.[50]

How far the motives for paternalistic activity extended beyond the instrumental idea that good management demanded the provision of incentives for employees is unclear.[51] Neither is it certain how widely paternalism was practised by cotton masters, nor how far it helped them to reduce industrial strife amongst their workers as the factory system developed. It has even been argued that cotton masters' actions were marked more by tyranny than by paternalism, the wrongs they perpetrated including the victimisation of employees holding radical political views, the imposition of frequent and severe fines for breach of mill rules and the implacable opposition they showed to trade unions. And it may also be the case that paternalism proved more influential during the mid-Victorian years when relationships

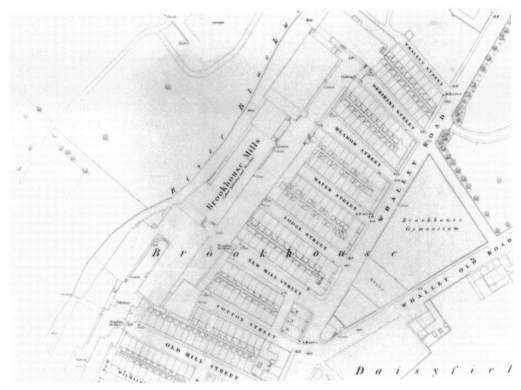

FIGURE 8. Brookhouse Mills, Blackburn, in the 1840s
This extract from the 1840s five feet to the mile OS map shows the mill colony founded by the Hornby family at Brookhouse, Blackburn. Facilities provided included a walled gymnasium.

between employers and employed became far less turbulent.[52] Much more research into these matters is plainly required.

Employers' sanctions could not prevent trade unionism developing amongst cotton operatives, however. Neither could such legal constraints as the Combination Acts of 1799–1824, which outlawed trade associations of both workers and employers, nor periodic depressions in trade, which reduced the ability of union members to pay their subscriptions. Yet union activities had often to take place under the guise of friendly societies, of which there were over 800 in Lancashire at the start of the nineteenth century.[53] Combinations of Lancashire textile workers had emerged by the mid-eighteenth century, the earliest involving cotton operatives probably being that of the check weavers. They sought to protect members' earnings by limiting numbers of new entrants into their trade and by resisting employers' attempts to increase the length of cloth for which a given price was paid. Faced with high food prices in the mid-1750s, they became more militant and during the summer of 1757, came out on strike throughout south-east Lancashire. Their employers resisted strongly, however, eventually taking legal proceedings against the leading union activists. The weavers did secure concessions regarding cloth lengths, but not over the 'charity boxes' into which members' subscriptions were paid. Employers did not believe that these existed solely to pay welfare benefits and required that they should be discontinued. As a result, the formal organisation of check weavers probably ceased, if only temporarily.[54]

Despite this early display of aggression, Lancashire's hand weavers seldom turned to industrial action. In part, this was because they comprised a large, varied and, to a marked extent, dispersed labour force, with the result that concerted action amongst them was difficult to achieve. It was also because hand weaving was a trade in which employers tended to own relatively little fixed capital, so that, compared with factory owners, they were less vulnerable to industrial action. Even so, they were able to organise widespread and sustained strikes in 1808, after the Commons failed to pass a minimum wage bill, and in 1818, as general strike action occurred amongst Lancashire workers. But the improvements achieved did not prove lasting and union activity could not prevent a long-term decline in hand weavers' piece rates.[55]

From the 1790s, meanwhile, local unions were also being formed amongst mule spinners, whose work was being speedily transferred into factories. By 1810, despite being illegal, these unions were organised into a countywide federation and were able to mount a lengthy strike in an attempt to standardise their wage rates at the highest prevailing level. They used the 'rolling strike' tactic, bringing out their members one mill or district at a time, so that strikers could be supported by the subscriptions of those still at work. The employers, though, were able to collaborate effectively and to inflict defeat by imposing a unified lock-out.[56]

Thereafter, the mule spinners faced an uphill struggle. They engaged in several major disputes, usually taking advantage of upturns in trade to maximise their bargaining power, as in 1818 and 1824–5.[57] Yet they continued to suffer crippling defeats, despite creating further federations amongst their own societies and co-ordinating their activities with those of the wider trade union movement. Both these tactics were employed during the late 1820s, with the formation of the Grand General Union of Cotton Spinners and the more broadly-based National Association for the Protection of Labour. They were inspired by John Doherty, one of the most outstanding amongst early trade unionists, but faced with economic recession, inadequate funding and internal rifts, as well as with determined resistance by employers' associations, there was little hope of success. In the event, both organisations proved short-lived and the strike action their members took did not prevent piece rate reductions.[58] As a result, spinners' average net earnings (allowing for payments to their piecers) are estimated to have fallen from 26–27s (£1.30–£1.35) per week in 1829 to 20–25s (£1.00–£1.25) in 1833. In percentage terms, this was by no means insignificant, though it still left spinners as the highest paid cotton operatives, as well as amongst the best paid workers in general.[59]

The spinners' problems in the early 1830s were compounded by the introduction of short-time working, as recession continued; by the appearance of the self-actor mule, which threatened to reduce their status as skilled workers and hence their earnings; and by the increasing tendency to install longer hand mules, which brought them lower piece rates and the prospect of fewer job opportunities. Their local societies remained in existence, though only the Oldham spinners took strike action, causing considerable disruption in the early months of 1834. However, as trade recovered during the mid-1830s, the Manchester spinners took the initiative in organising another federation of local spinning unions, this time to raise wages to the levels paid at

Bolton. Stoppages took place in several towns during 1836, the most serious being at Preston, where, in November, the association of millowners closed all their mills. But the strike was ill-timed, since recession had set in by the early months of 1837. Once more, severe defeat was imposed on the spinners. They did secure a temporary increase in wages, but, before being re-employed, they were forced to declare that they would abandon union involvement. Moreover, unemployment amongst them soon increased, both through the effects of the recession and through blacklisting of the most active strikers.[60]

References

1. P. Deane & W. A. Cole, *British Economic Growth, 1688–1959* (Cambridge University Press, 1962), pp. 185 & 187.

2. A. P. Wadsworth & J. de Lacy Mann, *The Cotton Trade and Industrial Lancashire, 1600–1780* (Manchester University Press, 1931), p. 170; M. M. Edwards, *The Growth of the British Cotton Trade, 1780–1815* (Manchester University Press, 1967), p. 8.

3. J. Holt, *General View of the Agriculture of the County of Lancaster* (London, 1795), p. 207.

4. For discussion, see Edwards, *Cotton Trade*, pp. 7–24.

5. See especially J. G. Williamson, 'Debating the Industrial Revolution', *Explorations in Economic History*, 24 (1987), pp. 269–92.

6. S. D. Chapman, *The Cotton Industry in the Industrial Revolution* (Macmillan, 1972), pp. 29–33 gives fixed capital figures for this period.

7. Wadsworth & de Lacy Mann, *Cotton Trade*, p. 142. One contemporary, though, mentions fustian printing at Manchester as early as 1700. See W. Farrer & J. Brownbill (eds), *A History of the County of Lancaster*, Pt 13 (London, 1920), pp. 395–7.

8. Parliamentary Papers, 1843 (431) XIV, *Children's Employment Commission, Appendix to Second Report*, Pt 1, pp. B2 & B3.

9. W. W. Rostow, *The Stages of Economic Growth* (Cambridge University Press, 1960), pp. 53–4.

10. For further discussion see Chapman, *Cotton Industry*, pp. 62–72.

11. Lancashire Record Office, *Blackburn Marriage Registers*, PR 3073/1/4 and *The Registers of the Parish Church of Croston* (Lancashire Parish Register Society, 1900), vol. 6. I am indebted to Tony Hart for providing the Croston figure. The 1813–17 figures can be found in J. G. Timmins, *The Decline of Handloom Weaving in Nineteenth-Century Lancashire* (PhD thesis, University of Lancaster, 1990), pp. 463.

12. For details see J. G. Timmins, *Handloom Weavers' Cottages in Central Lancashire* (Lancaster University Occasional Paper, 1977) and 'Handloom Weavers' Cottages in Central Lancashire: Some Problems of Recognition', *Post-Medieval Archaeology*, 13 (1979), pp. 251–72; and N. Morgan, *Vanished Dwellings* (Mullion Books, 1990).

13. G. Timmins, *The Last Shift* (Manchester University Press, 1993), pp. 57–9.

14. See, for example, E. Baines, *History of the Cotton Manufacture in Great Britain* (1835, reprinted Frank Cass, 1966), 147–63; W. English, *The Textile Industry* (Longmans, 1969), chs 7 & 8; Wadsworth and de Lacy Mann, *Cotton Trade*, pp. 476–85; H. Catling, *The Spinning Mule* (David and Charles, 1970), pp. 21–30; C. Aspin and S. D. Chapman, *James Hargreaves and the Spinning Jenny* (Helmshore Local History Society, 1965); and R. S. Fitton, *The Arkwrights: Spinners of Fortune* (Manchester University Press, 1989), ch. 2.

15. Catling, *Spinning Mule*, ch. 3; Baines, *Cotton Manufacture*, pp. 197–213; English, *Textile Industry*, ch. 9.

16. G. W. Daniels, 'Samuel Crompton's Census of the Cotton Industry in 1811', *Economic History*, (1930), pp. 107–8.

17. Catling, *Spinning Mule*, chs 4–6; English, *Textile Industry*, ch. 21; R. Marsden, *Cotton Spinning: Its Development, Principles and Practice* (London, 1886), pp. 289–90.

18. Timmins, *Last Shift*, p. 20 and ch. 4.

19. W. Radcliffe, *Origin of a New System of Manufacturing* (Stockport, 1828), pp. 18–31; R. Marsden, *Cotton Weaving: Its Development, Principles, and Practice* (London, 1895), pp. 328–33; D. Bythell, *The Handloom Weavers* (Cambridge University Press, 1969), p. 84.

20. Baines, *Cotton Manufacture*, pp. 264–8.

21. *Children's Employment Commission*, p. B3.

22. O. Ashmore, *Industrial Archaeology of Lancashire* (David & Charles, 1969), pp. 40–9.

23. R. Lloyd-Jones and M. Lewis, *Manchester and the Age of the Factory* (Croom Helm, 1988), p. 55.

24. A. Howe, *The Cotton Masters, 1830–1860* (Clarendon Press, 1984), pp. 3–6; V. A. C. Gatrell, 'Labour, Power and the Size of Firms in the Second Quarter of the Nineteenth Century', *Economic History Review*, 30 (1977), pp. 95–139; S. D. Chapman, 'Financial Restraints on the Growth of Firms in the Cotton Industry, 1790–1850', *Economic History Review*, 32 (1978) pp. 50–67.

25. For a discussion, see S. R. H. Jones, 'Technology, Transaction Costs, and the Transition to Factory Production in the British Silk Industry, 1700–1870', *Journal of Economic History*, 47 (1987), pp. 71–96; S. R. H. Jones, 'The origins of the factory system in Great Britain', in M. W. Kirby & M. B. Rose (eds), *British Enterprise in Modern Britain* (Routledge, 1994), pp. 31–64.

26. Catling, *Spinning Mule*, p. 54.

27. R. Bracegirdle, 'Textile Finishing in the North-West' in J. H. Smith (ed.), *The Great Human Exploit* (Phillimore, 1973), p. 37; Baines, *Cotton Manufacture*, p. 240.

28. Baines, *Cotton Manufacture*, pp. 247–53.

29. For discussion on pauper apprentices, see especially M. B. Rose, 'Social Policy and Business: Parish Apprenticeship and the Early Factory System, 1750–1834', *Business History*, 32 (1989), pp. 5–29; P. Horn, *Children's Work and Welfare, 1780–1880s* (Macmillan, 1994), pp. 29–40. On piecers,

see N. J. Smelser, *Social Change in the Industrial Revolution* (Routledge & Kegan Paul, 1959), pp. 189–90.

30. H. Cunningham, 'The Employment and Unemployment of Children in England, c.1680–1851', *Past and Present* (1990), pp. 115–50. See also C. Nardinelli, *Child Labor and the Industrial Revolution* (Indiana University Press, 1990), pp. 103–5.

31. Horn, *Children's Work*, pp. 50–8; Nardinelli, *Child Labor*, pp. 9–23. Contrasting contemporary views can be found, for example, in J. Fielden, *The Factory System* (1836, reprinted Frank Cass, 1969) and Baines, *Cotton Manufacture*, ch. 16. Nardinelli suggests there was a decline in the proportion of child labour used in cotton factories during the early decades of the nineteenth century, largely because improved mules needed fewer piecers and older workers were more available as cotton mills became urban based. See Nardinelli, *Child Labor*, pp. 105–18.

32. A. E. Peacock, 'The Successful Prosecution of the Factory, Acts, 1833–55', *Economic History Review*, 37 (1984), p. 201.

33. S. J. Chapman, *The Lancashire Cotton Industry* (Manchester University Press, 1904), pp. 93–4.

34. M. Anderson, *Family Structure in Nineteenth Century Lancashire* (Cambridge University Press, 1971), pp. 71–2.

35. For comment on this matter see J. Liddington and J. Norris, *One Hand Tied Behind Us* (Virago, 1984), ch. 3 and E. Roberts, *Women's Work, 1840–1940* (Macmillan, 1988), chs 1 & 4.

36. Edwards, *Cotton Trade*, chs 9 & 10; Chapman, *Cotton Industry*, pp. 37–42; R. Robson, *The Cotton Industry in Britain* (Macmillan, 1957), p. 31; F. Stuart Jones, 'The Financial Needs of the Cotton Industry During the Industrial Revolution: A Survey of Recent Research', *Textile History*, 16, (1985), pp. 45–67.

37. Lloyd-Jones & Lewis, *Age of the Factory*, pp. 45–6; A. Kidd, *Manchester* (Ryburn, 1993), pp. 23–5; Chapman, *Merchant Enterprise in Britain* (Cambridge University Press, 1992), pp. 172–5.

38. T. Ellison, *The Cotton Trade of Great Britain* (1886, reprinted Frank Cass, 1968), pp. 170–1 & 174–6; M. J. Power, 'The Growth of Liverpool' in J. Belchem (ed.), *Popular Politics, Riot and Labour* (Liverpool University Press, 1992), pp. 23–4; Farrer & Brownbill, *History*, pp. 392–3; Edwards, *Cotton Trade*, chs 5 & 6; Wadsworth & de Lacy Mann, *Cotton Trade*, pp. 183–92; Chapman, *Merchant Enterprise*, pp. 82–93.

39. Chapman, *Merchant Enterprise*, chs 2 & 6.

40. Edwards, *Cotton Trade*, pp. 25–9; Deane & Cole, *Economic Growth*, p. 187.

41. J. Mokyr (ed.), *The Economics of the Industrial Revolution* (George Allen & Unwin, 1985), p. 59.

42. For further discussion, see Edwards, *Cotton Trade*, pp. 29–48.

43. Deane & Cole, *Economic Growth*, p. 295; Chapman, *Cotton Industry*, p. 52.

44. D. A. Farnie, *The English Cotton Industry and the World Market, 1815–1896* (Clarendon Press, 1979), pp. 49–74 & 243.

45. K. Honeyman, *Origins of Enterprise* (Manchester University Press, 1982), pp. 55–82.

46. A. Howe, *The Cotton Masters, 1830–1860* (Clarendon Press, 1984), pp. 6–15.

47. Howe, Cotton Masters, pp. 61–72 & 87–9.

48. Wadsworth & de Lacy Mann, *Cotton Trade*, p. 307; Chapman, *Cotton Industry*, pp. 40 & 41.

49. W. Abram, *A History of Blackburn* (Blackburn, 1877), p. 405.

50. P. Joyce, *Work, Society and Politics* (Methuen, 1980), chs 6 & 7 especially; R. Boyson, *The Cotton Ashworth Enterprise* (Clarendon Press, 1970), chs 6 & 7; Walton, *Lancashire*, pp. 132–3; C. Aspin, *Lancashire, First Industrial Society* (Helmshore Local History Society, 1969), pp. 131–8.

51. S. Pollard, *The Genesis of Modern Management* (Penguin, 1965), pp. 231–44.

52. H. I. Dutton & J. E. King, 'The Limits of Paternalism: the Cotton Tyrants of North Lancashire, 1836–54', *Social History*, 7 (1982), pp. 59–74; Aspin, *Lancashire*, pp. 66–87.

53. A. Fowler & T. Wyke, *The Barefoot Aristocrats* (Kessall, 1987), pp. 14–17; Walton, *Lancashire*, p. 143.

54. Wadsworth & de Lacy Mann, *Cotton Trade*, pp. 340–75.

55. Bythell, *Handloom Weavers*, pp. 143–5.

56. Walton, *Lancashire*, pp. 145–6; Fowler & Wyke, *Aristocrats*, pp. 18–23.

57. For discussion of this important point, see A. E. Musson, *British Trade Unions, 1800–1875* (Macmillan, 1972), pp. 38–48.

58. Walton, Lancashire, pp. 146–7; Fowler & Wyke, *Aristocrats*, pp. 28–35; H. A. Turner, *Trade Union Growth, Structure and Policy* (Allen & Unwin, 1962), pp. 99–104; R. G. Kirby & A. E. Musson, *The Voice of the People* (Manchester University Press, 1975); Chapman, *Lancashire Cotton*, pp. 180–206.

59. Kirby & Musson, *Voice*, p. 146.

60. Kirby & Musson, *Voice*, pp. 272–308; Fowler & Wyke, *Aristocrats*, p. 33.

CHAPTER THREE

The rise to the peak years

c.1840–1914

Growth and fluctuations in output

 hroughout this period, the Lancashire cotton industry continued to expand at a remarkable rate. Retained raw cotton imports again provide a useful measure, their annual average rising almost fivefold, from 452 million lbs (205 thousand tonnes) in 1839–41 to 2,132 million lbs (967 thousand tonnes) in 1912–14. They never attained such a high level again, so that the industry's peak output figures belong to these years.[1]

The industry did not maintain its rate of growth, however. Thus, whereas raw cotton imports increased at an annual average of 7.4 per cent between 1780 and 1840, they averaged a rise of only 3.3 per cent per annum between 1840 and 1872 and as little as 1.4 per cent per annum between 1872 and 1913. With such a marked fall in its long-term growth rate, the industry's relative importance in the national economy declined appreciably. During the 1860s and early 1870s, it contributed more than 11 per cent to the gross value of UK output; by 1901, however, this figure had shrunk to 5.4 per cent. The industry's share of UK employment held up rather better during these years, but still fell from 4.1 per cent to 3.3 per cent.[2]

In addition to these long-term changes in the industry's growth, there were also the inevitable short-term fluctuations associated with trade-cycle movements. As in earlier times, these could bring periods of high prosperity as well as of deep

45

depression. During the early 1870s, for example, one of the most prosperous periods ever to arise in the industry occurred. It resulted partly from a general surge in the economy, but also from a sharp rise in demand for British cottons because of disruption to continental textile production during the Franco-Prussian War.[3] A further boom occurred in 1905–7, increasing average spinning company profits from £7,701 to £13,211 and encouraging the industry's last wave of mill building.[4]

As to periods of depression, the most severe in the industry's history occurred during the Cotton Famine of the early and mid-1860s. Once attributed to a shortage of raw cotton during the American Civil War, the Famine is now regarded as a response to a massive over-production of textile goods that arose in the late 1850s and early 1860s. By November, 1862, when the depression was at its most acute, cotton operatives were working only 2⅓ days per week on average compared with the six days to which they were accustomed.

The impact of the Famine on Lancashire people varied. Towns which depended less heavily on the cotton trade enjoyed a measure of immunity and even those that were at first badly hit were able to adapt with some success to changing market conditions. At Blackburn, for example, the production of bordered dhotis (loincloths) for the Indian market was successfully introduced. Meanwhile an extensive relief programme was implemented, which included distribution of food, clothes and fuel (PLATE 14), the implementation of public works projects and the establishment of adult education classes.

Yet, despite these measures, distress was real. All too many cotton operatives were forced to reduce their savings and sell or pawn their possessions. They could not afford to buy the usual amount or variety of food, with bread, oatmeal porridge and potatoes forming their staple diet. And overcrowding became more prevalent as efforts were made to save on rent and fuel. Consequently, higher levels of ill-health developed, with women proving especially susceptible.[5]

Localisation and specialisation in cotton production

The localisation of cotton production in Lancashire intensified during the Victorian period. In 1838, nearly 60 per cent of the nation's cotton operatives were to be found in the county, a

PLATE 14. Cotton Famine relief scenes.
The engravings show coal being distributed at the Old Coal Wharf, Castlefield, Manchester and the shop for mill operatives at Birley's Mill, Manchester.
Source: *The Illustrated London News*, 6.12.1862.

figure that totalled over 80 per cent when those in adjoining districts of Cheshire, Derbyshire and Yorkshire are also considered. By the end of the century, these figures had respectively reached 76 per cent and 91 per cent[6] (FIGURE 9). Such a remarkable degree of concentration resulted partly from the fuller exploitation of the region's natural and acquired locational advantages. But it also arose from the decline of cotton production in the Clyde Valley, the other major centre of the industry. Here, the number of cotton employees fell from 35,600 in 1838 to 29,000 in 1898–9, as the locational advantages the area possessed for engineering, especially shipbuilding, were increasingly realised and it became harder for the cotton industry to obtain the labour and capital it needed.[7]

The concentration of cotton production in eastern and central Lancashire was reinforced by the industry's growing use of

FIGURE 9. Growing concentration of cotton production in Lancashire, 1838 (top) 1898–9 (bottom).
Source: W. Farrer & J. Brownbill (eds), *A History of the County of Lancaster* Pt 13 (Constable & Co., 1920), p. 382.

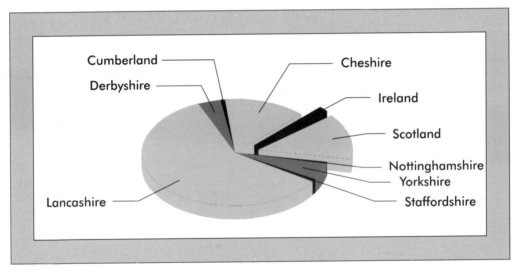

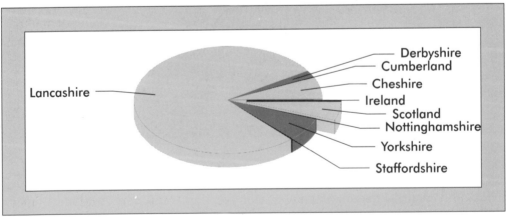

steam power. From the outset, the industry had been largely centred on the coalfield, the Preston and the Ribble Valley areas eventually emerging as the main exceptions.[8] Accordingly, as steam power grew to prominence in the industry from the late eighteenth century onwards, and coal therefore became the main power source, the cost of transporting it was kept to a minimum.

Within this area, the industry continued to develop much more strongly in urban than in rural locations. Indeed, factory colonies comprised a major element in the growth of Lancashire's cotton towns.[9] From the businessman's viewpoint, locating in a town rather than a rural district brought several advantages, including easier access to labour, housing and communications. Even so, some urban cotton masters were willing to incur the expense of providing housing and other facilities for their work-people, perhaps as a means of exerting control over them.

A final locational change that must be noted was a move towards sub-regional specialisation in different branches of the trade. One dimension of this was the tendency, by no means clear-cut, for spinning to become concentrated in the south-east of the county, whilst powerloom weaving developed most strongly in the towns to the north (FIGURE 10). This was

FIGURE 10 (below and overleaf). Geographical distribution of spinning and weaving, 1901.
Source: W. Farrer & J. Brownbill (eds), *A History of the County of Lancaster* Pt 13 (Constable & Co., 1920), p. 392.

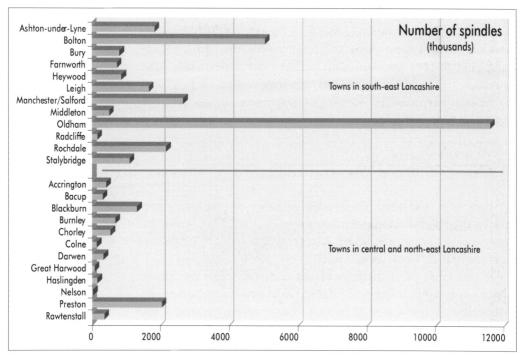

49

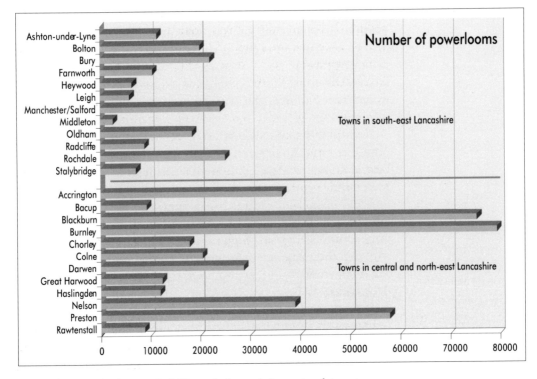

Number of powerlooms

Towns in south-east Lancashire

Towns in central and north-east Lancashire

associated with the availability of cheap labour in the area at a time when the powerloom was gaining ascendancy.[10] The other dimension was that towns increasingly concentrated on particular products. In the spinning area, for example, Oldham became associated with coarse yarns and Bolton with fine yarns.[11] Such a high degree of specialisation reflects the remarkable size to which the industry grew and the wide range of products it offered. This enabled firms to concentrate on goods of a particular type and quality.

Changes in the size and structure of firms

Between 1850 and 1890, the average number of employees per firm in the English cotton trade showed a notable increase. In the spinning branch, the figure rose from 106 to 155 and in the weaving branch from 98 to 173.[12]

For the most part, these increases occurred from the 1870s when a growing number of large-scale producers emerged, particularly in the spinning branch. They were encouraged by legislation passed in the 1840s and 1850s, which was consolidated by the Companies Act of 1862. This eased the formation of joint-stock companies, so that finance could be raised by selling shares and debentures (loan stock) to outside investors. And it gave investors limited liability, so that they could not be held responsible for a firm's debts beyond the value of their investment in it. By the mid-1890s, over a thousand joint-stock companies had been formed in the cotton industry. Half were in the spinning trade, and Oldham, which became the world's major spinning town during the 1860s, emerged as the main centre for them. Here, around 15 per cent of total flotations occurred, over half of which, a much higher proportion than was usual, were concerned with new mill construction.[13]

The emergence of joint-stock financing also paved the way for cotton firms to grow through amalgamation. Indeed, mergers became a characteristic feature in British manufacturing industry during the late nineteenth and early twentieth centuries, with the textile trades to the fore. As far as Lancashire firms were concerned, the most notable amongst them were the Fine Cotton Spinners' and Doublers' Association (1898), the Calico Printers' Association (1899), the British Cotton and Wool Dyers' Association (1900) and the Bleachers' Association (1900). The mergers aimed to curb the intense competition that had developed in certain sections of the industry as sales became harder to achieve. The resultant firms were as impressive in size as they were in the degree of control they achieved over output. Thus, the Calico Printers' Association was formed from 59 firms controlling some 85 per cent of the country's calico printing and had an initial capital of £9.2 million. As was common with these mergers, the services of former proprietors were retained, so that, incredibly, a board of directors with no fewer than 84 members was created, of whom 8 were managing directors.[14]

The move towards larger-scale production amongst spinning firms was accompanied by the installation of longer self-acting mules and the introduction of more efficient power transmission using the rope-race (PLATE 15). By the 1890s, huge mills with 100,000 mule spindles were becoming standard.[15] They emerged as a ubiquitous and dominant landscape feature, their steel-frame construction allowing a remarkably high ratio of window to wall space, thereby providing good natural lighting. And, compared with most earlier mills, they were built to be visually impressive, full opportunity being taken to incorporate ornate decoration and varied building materials[16] (PLATE 16).

Despite the growing number of large-scale concerns, small and medium-sized firms remained the most numerous. They were

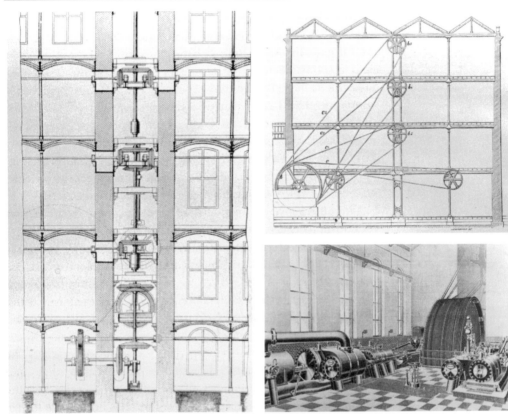

PLATE 15. Transmission of power in mills.

The first illustration shows how power was transmitted using gears and shafting at India Mill, Darwen, erected in 1868. The second is of a mill in which the transmission of power was by belts and pulleys. The belts were driven from a drum (b) about 15 feet (4.6 metres) in diameter. Belts were quieter and easier to maintain than gearing.

The belt drive system was improved by the use of rope drives. As the illustration shows, the ropes ran from a grooved flywheel powered by a horizontal steam engine.

Sources: Evan Leigh, *The Science of Modern Cotton Spinning* (Manchester, 1873), p. 40 & PLATE XIII, and J. Nasmith, *Recent Cotton Mill Construction and Engineering* (1894), p. 203.

encouraged by ease of entry into the industry, not least because newcomers could rent premises, power and machinery, and by the availability of both long and short-term credit. Moreover, they were often content to remain of limited size, perhaps only earning modest profits, and, all too frequently, were forced out of business before they were able to expand.[17]

The smaller cotton firms during this period generally special-ised in one of the industry's three main processes – spinning, weaving or finishing – rather than operating as integrated concerns. In fact, integrated firms, which mostly combined

PLATE 16. Imperial Mill, Blackburn. This striking example of a late cotton spinning mill was built in 1900–1. As the photograph reveals, it is a four-storeyed structure, its north wall comprising seventeen bays, each with three window openings. At both ends is an ornate water-tank tower, capped by a copper dome. The mill is fire-proofed, the ceilings of each storey consisting of arched, brick roofs which support concrete floors. (Photograph courtesy of Mike Rothwell.)

spinning with weaving, probably reached their greatest importance during the second quarter of the century. By 1850, they comprised nearly one-third of England's factory-based cotton firms, possessing over half the spindles, more than 60 per cent of the labour force and an impressive 83 per cent of power-looms. By 1890, however, as the small-scale, specialist firm prospered, they were reduced to fewer than one-fifth of the total, with under a third of the spindles, 38 per cent of employees and 42 per cent of looms.[18] Explanations for these changes centre on the huge growth in demand for cotton goods during the second half of the nineteenth century, which greatly stimulated each major sector of the industry and reduced the need for firms to integrate. They had previously done so for defensive reasons, with the spinners seeking to guarantee a market for at least part of their yarn output, to open up additional markets through cloth sales and, despite incurring only a modest outlay on looms, to spread fixed costs over a greater volume of output.[19]

The demise of handloom weaving

The decisive shift in the balance between hand and power weaving in Lancashire took place during the 1840s. It owed much to fundamental improvements in the powerloom during the early years of the decade. These were associated with William

Kenworthy and James Bullough of Blackburn and included an effective weft-stop motion. This halted the loom when a weft thread broke or the shuttle pirn became empty. As a result, weavers could operate more than one loom with far greater ease.[20]

The progress made by the powerloom during the 1840s was also assisted by a major upturn in the trade cycle. This occurred during the middle years of the decade, encouraging a massive expansion of existing capacity. Indeed, of the 100,000 or so additional powerlooms that were installed in Lancashire factories between 1835 and 1850, the bulk belonged to this period.[21] As a result, single-storey weaving sheds, with their characteristic saw-toothed roofs, became increasingly common. The glazed sections of the roofs usually faced north – or as near north as was practicable – and were angled steeply enough to prevent sunlight shining directly into the shed, an important matter in weaving coloured cloths[22] (PLATE 17).

Despite such impressive investment levels, the powerloom did not immediately supersede the handloom. It is true that the number of hand weavers in Lancashire fell substantially during the 1840s, with perhaps as many as 100,000 leaving the trade, especially in towns. Yet counts using 1851 census data suggest that around 55,000 were still to be found in the county, about two-thirds of whom worked with cotton and most of the remainder with silk or mixed-fibres. A decade later, Lancashire's hand weavers still numbered around 30,000, of whom around half produced cotton goods. Even as late as 1871, around 10,000 Lancashire hand weavers remained and it was not until the

PLATE 17a. Powerloom weaving shed. The weaving shed shown in this photograph forms part of Hilden Manufacturing Company's Oswaldtwistle Mills. It is no longer used for weaving.

PLATE 17b. Power-loom weaving shed. This photograph of the interior of Hilden Manufacturing Company's Oswaldtwistle Mills demonstrates the evenness of the lighting that could be attained with roof windows.

following decade that hand weaving in the county became virtually extinct.[23]

Hand weaving proved so durable partly because powerlooms did not always turn out to be efficient, even after the advances that were made during the early 1840s. This was especially so with regard to the production of fine and fancy wares. Additionally, manufacturers might decide to retain at least some hand weavers to meet abnormal or specialist demand for their products. The former arose periodically as the trade cycle peaked; the latter resulted from frequent changes in consumer preferences, which could require short production runs of higher-quality cloths.

In addition to these considerations, manufacturers also had to bear in mind the extra wage, machinery and equipment costs they would incur by transferring to powerlooms. These might be at least partly offset by saving on the costs of domestic production, including theft of yarn and transportation of materials between warehouse and home. And the closer supervision of weavers that could be achieved in factories might also help to raise both the level and quality of output. Moreover, higher profits might be anticipated from the use of powerlooms. Even so, this was by no means assured and those favouring powerloom investment had to bear in mind that, during trade recessions, the cost of fixed capital would still have to be met, even though it might be appreciably under-used. Accordingly, to invest in powerlooms might add considerably to business risks.

That cotton manufacturers long had the option of retaining hand technology was made possible by the persistence of a sizeable body of domestic weavers. This was partly the result of the technical inadequacies of the powerloom and of the problems hand weavers experienced in finding other types of employment. But there was also a desire within hand weaving communities to preserve a traditional way of life. This might

PLATE 17c. Interior of powerloom weaving shed.
This photograph, taken at Old Hall Mill, Dukinfield, around 1900, shows a weaving shed fitted with plain looms. Not all of the shed appears to have had roof lights, or, at least, roof lights that all faced the same direction. Notable features are the unprotected drive belts to the looms and the elevated line shafts and pulleys that transmitted power from the steam engine. Source: W. Burnett Tracy, *Port of Manchester* (Manchester, 1901).

not have yielded a high family income, but it did give a large measure of freedom from work supervision and allowed family working groups to continue.[24]

Supply-side aspects in the growth of the industry

The key advances made in powerloom technology during the early 1840s were subjected to numerous refinements in subsequent decades, as patent specifications reveal.[25] Such advances helped further to improve the productivity of weavers, which rose by an annual average of 2.7 per cent from 1850–73 and, despite a fall thereafter, by an average of over 1 per cent per

annum from 1884–96. These improvements are revealed in the
greater number of looms per operative, with four-loom weavers
becoming increasingly common. Moreover, technical advance
allowed finer and fancier grades of cloth to be woven on the
powerloom. Particularly notable here is the the dobby, or small
Jacquard. Introduced during the late 1850s, it provided a means
by which patterned cloth, including that for dhotis, could be
woven automatically.[26]

In the spinning branch of the industry, much innovative effort
during this period was devoted to improving the efficiency of
the mule, with increases in both the speed of spindles and the
number of spindles per machine. Self-actor mules became prominent, too. Even at Bolton, the main centre for fine spinning,
their numbers almost equalled those of hand-assisted mules by
1877.[27] And innovation also occurred as ring spinning was
adopted, albeit to a limited extent (PLATE 18). Unlike the mule,
the ring-frame spun continuously and needed only unskilled
labour. As in weaving, such innovation helped to improve productivity, the annual average for spinners rising 2.1 per cent
from 1850–73 and 1.6 per cent from 1873–96.[28]

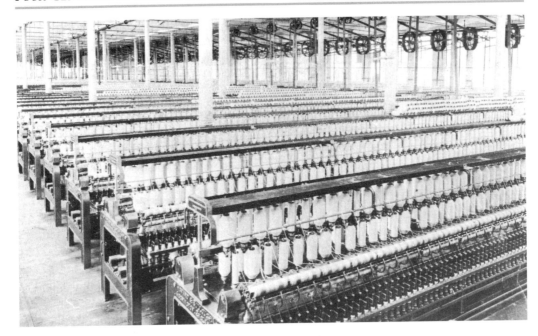

With regard to the finishing trades, hand printing with blocks diminished in importance as cylinder printing became capable of producing more complex patterns. Additionally, both dyeing and printing were stimulated by the introduction of synthetic or coal-tar dyestuffs. They dated from the 1850s, eventually making a wide range of colours available to the industry and requiring only a fraction of the amount of natural dye to process a given quantity of material.[29]

The growing use of more efficient powered machinery made cotton manufacturing less labour intensive. Nevertheless, the scale of its development ensured that it continued to make heavy demands on the labour force. The 1911 census for Lancashire records no fewer than 444,213 people employed in cotton production, almost one in five of the total workforce. In the cotton towns, the proportion could reach more than half.[30] Female labour was especially important, rising from 48 per cent of the industry total in 1835 to nearly 61 per cent in 1913 (FIGURE 11). This was partly a result of rising wages for women and the more stringent limits on the hours they could legally work, which were reduced from 69 per week in 1844 to 55.5 in 1901. But it may also have resulted from a fall in the use of child labour, the proportion of under 14s in the industry dropping from 13.1 per cent in 1835 to 3.2 per cent in 1907. The progress made in limiting children's working hours, and in

PLATE 18b. Ring frames.
This photograph shows ring spinning frames at Imperial Mill, Blackburn. The process made use of rollers for drafting, the threads being twisted by C-shaped rings (travellers) running around the perimeters of circular holes. (Photograph courtesy of Mike Rothwell.)

PLATES 18c & 18d. Self-cleaning carding engines.

Major improvements were also made in the preparatory stages of spinning with the development of the self-cleaning carding engine. A continuous chain of card strips (or flats) revolved above the main carding cylinder. They both turned in the same direction, the flats at a much slower rate. The roller brush at the front of the machine (above the flats) cleaned loose fibres from the flats. Operatives complained of the dust this type of carding machine produced, however. Source: W. Burnett Tracy, *Port of Manchester* (Manchester, 1901).

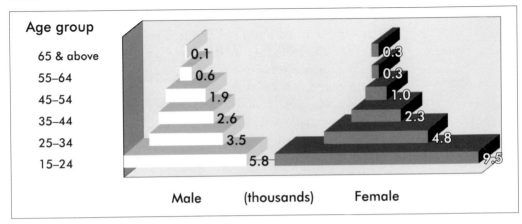

Age group		
65 & above	0.1	0.3
55–64	0.6	0.3
45–54	1.9	1.0
35–44	2.6	2.3
25–34	3.5	4.8
15–24	5.8	9.5

Male   (thousands)   Female

extending their educational opportunities, strongly influenced this development.[31]

It was not only the availability of labour, however, that was important in helping to promote the industry's growth and maintain its competitiveness. So, too, was the range of skills and depth of experience it could offer. Additionally, it was a labour force accustomed to the long hours and steady pace that factory work required, as well as being confident that its piece rates would not be cut when more effort was expended to increase earnings. These arguments need fuller consideration than can be given here, but issues concerning labour quality must be duly recognised.[32]

In seeking finance to expand the industry, heavy reliance continued to be made on partnerships and re-invested profits, despite the rise of share financing by joint-stock companies. Indeed, the impact of share sales in providing finance for the cotton industry should not be overstated. This is partly because it was more prevalent in some towns than in others, with Oldham, Rochdale and Ashton-under-Lyne being to the fore in Lancashire. Moreover, about one-third of joint-stock companies were private limited concerns, which did not extend share ownership beyond a small circle of partners and family members. Nor, except at Oldham and Darwen, did it become common for joint-stock companies either to sell small-denomination shares to local people, or to accept small loans from them. Only to a limited extent, therefore, did joint-stock companies democratise the cotton industry and free it from the need to tap its traditional sources of finance.[33]

As in earlier times, development of the region's infrastructure played a key role in enabling the industry to expand. Particularly

FIGURE 11. Age and gender of textile operatives in Oldham, 1911.
In 1911, 56 per cent of Oldham's textile workers (the vast majority being in the cotton industry) were female. Young workers predominated, their importance being enhanced when those in the 10–14 age group are also taken into account. They totalled 3,582 and 2,100 of them (59 per cent) were girls.
Source: *Census of England and Wales*, 1911.

important was the completion of the railway network. This greatly enhanced the speed and frequency of transport services, so that entrepreneurs in the manufacturing towns had much easier and quicker access to commercial facilities at Manchester and Liverpool.[34] And these facilities were greatly extended. Thus, Manchester continued to develop its traditional function in marketing cotton goods, its central area becoming increasingly dominated by imposing, visually-impressive warehouses (PLATE 19). Here, too, was the cotton exchange, periodically rebuilt to accommodate ever-growing numbers of traders.[35] At Liverpool, meanwhile, major dock extensions took place, enabling vastly-increased amounts of raw cotton imports and cotton goods exports to be handled. However, trade was lost to Manchester following the opening of the Manchester Ship Canal in 1894 (PLATE 20). Indeed, by 1900, over half a million bales of raw cotton per year were being shipped up the Canal, appreciably reducing the freight and port charges that Manchester's business community had long regarded as excessive.[36] Nor should it be overlooked that substantial benefits continued to be derived from the growth of ancillary industries, especially textile machinery and equipment makers. They supplied spare parts as well as new machines, often on credit, and were to be found in most of the textile towns. Some operated on a substantial scale, the giant of the industry, Platt Brothers of Oldham, having no fewer than 10,000 employees in 1910. These firms also developed an extensive export trade, thereby assisting the growth of competitor textile industries.[37]

PLATE 19. Horrockses, Crewdson & Co.'s warehouse, Piccadilly, Manchester.
By the mid-Victorian years, cotton firms' warehouses were becoming concentrated in the southern part of Manchester's central business district. They were used to display and sell goods by sample, as well as for storage. Accordingly, as in the case of the building shown, they were intended to be visually striking, often being designed by leading architects. Source: W. Burnett Tracy, *Port of Manchester* (Manchester, 1901).

PLATE 20. Transporting cotton along the Manchester Ship Canal.
This photograph records the first cargo of cotton carried along the Canal to be unloaded at Manchester in January 1894. The cargo, comprising 4,170 bales, was unloaded by mobile cranes.
Source: W. Burnett Tracy, *Port of Manchester* (Manchester, 1901).

Demand-side aspects in the growth of the industry

Throughout this period, export demand remained crucial to the growth of the cotton industry. In 1839–41, the annual average volume of yarn and cloth exports stood at 452 million lbs (205 thousand tonnes) a figure which rose more than threefold to reach 1,444 million lbs (655 thousand tonnes) by 1912–14, despite something of a reduction in yarn exports from the late 1880s.[38] It is true that, by mid-century, cotton goods had passed their maximum proportion of the country's total export value. Nonetheless, they continued to rise as a proportion of the industry's total production. Thus, between 1844–46 they averaged 55.4 per cent of output value, but increased to no less than 78.8 per cent from 1899–1901.[39] This is more impressive given the high tariff barriers they faced in Europe and the United States.

The level of sales continued to rise in each of the established overseas markets, except for the United States. In volume terms, sales of cotton piece goods to that country halved between 1850 and 1896, though in terms of value they remained little changed. Plainly, United States cotton manufacturers were increasingly able to meet the needs of domestic consumers, though less fully with regard to higher-value goods, considerable quantities of which still had to be imported.[40]

The most notable development, though, was the emergence of Asia, especially India, as the predominant market for British cotton exports. The growing sales to this region before mid-century have already been noted and they continued to rise thereafter. They were channelled through 'agency houses', which increasingly traded on their own account and invested locally. By the mid-1890s, India was taking 39 per cent by volume of cotton piece-goods exports and 27 per cent by value of cotton manufactures exports (FIGURE 6, page 35). Cheap, unfinished calicoes predominated. Despite their immense volume, British imports by no means displaced India's cotton manufacturers, who bought cheap yarn from Britain and continued to produce muslins of the highest quality.[41]

A failure of entrepreneurship?

It has been seen that, despite its impressive growth throughout the nineteenth century, the cotton industry became relatively less important in the British economy from the 1870s onwards. During the same period, as overseas competition intensified, its international importance also declined. Thus, with regard to cotton piece-goods, it provided 82 per cent of world trade in 1882–4, compared with 70 per cent in 1910–3.[42]

In part, the growing competition from overseas resulted from the success of established producers in the United States and continental Europe. But it also arose as other countries established factory-based cotton industries. They included India in the 1850s and Japan by the 1870s. Indeed, it was the rise of these industries which led to a marked reduction in Britain's exports of cotton yarn during the 1880s and 1890s.[43]

In seeking explanations for the relative decline of the British cotton industry and, for that matter, other British industries, the notion of inadequate entrepreneurship has been posited.[44] As far as the cotton industry is concerned, the alleged failings have been perceived in terms of attitudes towards technological innovation. Compared with their overseas competitors, British cotton producers were slow to adopt not only ring-frames, but also automatic looms, which replenished the weft without stopping (PLATE 21). In the United States, for example, mule spinning had been largely abandoned in favour of ring spinning by the outbreak of World War I, whereas in Britain, there were still over four times as many mule as ring spindles. As a result, American

PLATE 21. Automatic looms.
The illustration is of a pair of early automatic looms. The circular magazines contain full pirns (small diameter cotton bobbins) which were transferred directly into the shuttle when it became empty. The boxes beneath the magazines caught the empty pirns as they were ejected from the shuttle. The looms are 'lefts' or 'rights' according to the position of the magazines and boxes.
Source: Draper, *Labor Saving Looms* (Hopedale, 1904), p. 76.

producers could take advantage of cheap, unskilled labour and of machines which, because they spun continuously rather than intermittently, could produce a third more yarn per spindle.[45]

That the tardiness of British cotton employers in re-equipping amounts to a failure of entrepreneurship does not have unqualified support, however. Counter-argument suggests that most were acting rationally in persevering with mules and semi-automatic (plain) looms. By developing the full potential of these machines, they were, after all, able to raise output and, until the 1890s at least, productivity. As well, savings from using ring-frames arose only with coarser yarns, in which Britain had less interest than her competitors. It has also been argued that investment in ring-frames and automatic looms was the more difficult because of the structure of the industry, with spinning and weaving tending to be undertaken by specialist firms located in different parts of the county. Both groups would have needed to re-equip given the incompatibility of mule yarn with automatic looms and ring-frame yarn with semi-automatic (plain) looms. And even if they had, ring-frame yarn, which was wound on to wooden bobbins, was more costly to transport than mule yarn, which was wound on to paper tubes or the bare spindle. Moreover, traditional machines brought economies because they were more effective than new ones with low-quality fibres. This was because the intermittent action of the mule reduced strain on the yarn during spinning, whilst the higher breakage rate of inferior yarn was more costly when expensive automatic looms were used.[46]

Disagreement remains about aspects of the debate, including whether the industry's productivity rose after 1890 and whether Britain's cotton producers were reluctant to re-equip because of the industry's structure or because they had a strong preference for mules.[47] Yet, as attempts have been made to rehabilitate the entrepreneur, discussion has broadened to consider why Britain dominated world cotton manufacturing before World War I and lost the lead thereafter. The argument has been formulated in terms of changing comparative advantage. Thus, it is suggested that British cotton firms in the pre-war decades had several advantages over their rivals, namely a more productive labour force, easier access to skilled labour for maintaining machinery, machines that could be used economically with varying grades of cotton, a more sophisticated marketing system and lower administrative costs arising with specialist as opposed to integrated firms.[48]

Developments in trade unionism and employers' associations

Recovery of the spinners' unions from the defeats of the late 1830s was hampered by several years of recession. For a time, industrial action gave way to support for political reform, as many textile operatives turned to Chartism. But by 1842, a further attempt was made to co-ordinate local spinners' societies with the formation of the Operative Cotton Spinners of Lancashire, Cheshire, Yorkshire and Derbyshire. During the mid-1840s, the Society encouraged districts to seek wage advances, which, as the economy boomed, were widely conceded, and it became active in pressing for the Ten Hours Bill, which was effectively secured in 1850. More successful than earlier associations, its existence was nonetheless sorely threatened by trade recession and internal division during the late 1840s, when wage-cutting and unemployment again ensued.[49]

For a time, trade union activity in spinning reverted to the local societies, which became particularly active in 1853. By then, though, their Association had revived and, with a strong upsurge in the trade cycle, a campaign to restore the wage cuts of the late 1840s was mounted. It involved weavers as well as spinners and success was quickly achieved in several districts. At Preston, however, a well-established association of cotton masters held out, sustained by subscriptions from employers in other towns and by binding themselves to pay a sum of no less than £5,000 should they fail to abide by the decisions of their association. After a seven-month lockout, union members were forced to return without any wage increase.[50]

One key advance made during the early 1850s was the establishment in north-east Lancashire of a standard wage list. Known as the Blackburn List, it was jointly agreed by employers and operative spinners and weavers, setting a price for a standard job and making allowance for such variables as quality of product. Local lists of this type had long been in use,[51] but the stipulation that future disputes should be brought before a committee of masters and men pointed to a new era in which joint negotiation would become an accepted feature of industrial relations.[52] This is not to suggest that the cotton industry was free from major strikes and lock-outs beyond the mid-nineteenth century. However, it has been argued that attitudes of employers and employed changed, the former ceasing to regard trade unions as 'organised insubordination' and the latter to view associations of employers as 'malevolent combinations of their oppressors'.[53]

Yet the argument must be qualified, at least with regard to the mid-Victorian period, when anti-union feeling seems to have been stronger amongst employers who paid low wages than amongst those who paid high wages. The latter, it is suggested, tolerated and even encouraged trade unions as a means of equalising wages between districts. This helped to ensure that the cost advantage of the former was minimised. Conversely, the low wage payers were opposed to unions and uniform wage lists, since both helped to prevent wage cuts.

The way these differences emerged can be seen in the case of the 1853–4 strike at Preston. Preston employers paid lower wages than their Blackburn neighbours, who had anyway conceded the 10 per cent rise that was being generally sought. This was seen as bad enough, but the Blackburn employers were also chastised for not giving financial support to help in breaking the Preston strike and for allowing their employees to send funds to the Preston strikers. In fact, it was employers in the lower-wage areas of the county, including Rossendale and Burnley, who most actively supported the Preston masters.[54]

The issue of controlling competition within the industry became increasingly important during the later decades of the nineteenth century. By then, overseas competitors were emerging strongly, with the result that the industry's profitability was much reduced, especially in spinning.[55] Accordingly, employers formed more widely-based associations. These aimed at preventing competitive price cutting amongst members, which would reduce profitability further. Additionally, they sought to curb the growing power of trade unions, particularly with regard to demands for wage increases. This policy was helped by further development of standard wage lists, three of which had become widely adopted by the 1890s. They were the Uniform List in weaving (an amalgamation of the Blackburn, Preston and Burnley lists), the Oldham List in coarse spinning, and the Bolton List in fine spinning.[56]

Amongst the employers' associations, two grew to prominence. The earlier, the North and North-East Lancashire Cotton Spinners' and Manufacturers' Association, was formed in 1866 and by 1914, it represented firms owning 61 per cent of the Lancashire weaving capacity. The other was the Federation of Master Cotton Spinners' Associations. Formed as late as 1891, it absorbed the Bolton fine spinners in 1905, and by 1914 had federated firms owning 64 per cent of Lancashire's spinning capacity.[57]

Meanwhile, operatives' organisations also developed. The mule spinners led the way, finally creating a permanent organisation in 1870, when the Amalgamated Association of Operative Spinners and Twiners was founded. Their motive was not only to improve their bargaining strength, but also to provide a more effective means of promoting political demands in parliament. In weaving, the various local societies that had sprung up during the early Victorian years were partially amalgamated in 1858, but they did not manage a countywide federation until their Second Amalgamation was formed in 1884.[58]

The objectives of the two organisations differed appreciably. Thus, the mule spinners' union, exclusively male, aimed particularly to maintain the skilled status of its members and the high wage differentials they enjoyed. Accordingly, it continued to press for limits to the number of piecers per spinner and for piecers to stay within the spinners' union. They also sought to maintain payment of piece-rates to spinners and time-rates to piecers, so that benefits of extra piece-rate earnings went to spinners. Thus, as production rates improved, wage costs per unit of ouput were reduced, providing a further incentive for employers to stick with mules.[59]

With substantial funding from high subscription rates and a growing, but by no means complete willingness to negotiate and compromise rather than take strike action, the spinners achieved considerable success. Thus, in such places as Oldham and Rochdale, agreements were made that the number of piecers per spinner should be limited to two, so that entry into the trade was effectively restricted, whilst in 1876, spinners' piece-rates and piecers' time-rates were linked to the Oldham List, thereby maintaining the differentials between them. Moreover, following a twenty-week lock-out in 1892–3, when the spinners were able to limit a threatened 5 per cent wage reduction to one of 2.9 per cent, the Brooklands' Agreement was implemented. This stipulated that wage rates could only be varied at yearly intervals and by not more than 5 per cent. It also introduced formal conciliation procedures.[60] Unfortunately, the Agreement did not allow compensation for the more frequent yarn breakages that occurred when cheaper yarns were used, the so-called 'bad spinning'. This became a growing problem as cotton firms economised on raw material costs in the decades leading up to World War I, contributing to more strained industrial relations and prompting the spinners to withdraw from the Agreement in 1913.[61]

In contrast to the spinners' association, that of the weavers' was far less exclusive. Operating with low subscription rates, its membership grew rapidly, reaching nearly 200,000 by 1914. Since it could not hope to raise wages through achieving skilled status for its members, its key aim was to maintain standard piece-rate lists, which would prevent wage reductions by individual employers. But it also campaigned against such practices as 'driving' – paying output commission to overlookers, which could result in excessive pressure being placed on weavers; 'steaming' – creating high humidity in weaving sheds to help produce low-grade cloth, which meant weavers worked in unhealthy conditions; and 'time cribbing' – increasing production by starting a few minutes before the official time and continuing a little beyond it.[62]

Finally, union development in the preparatory processes must be noted. The Association of Card, Blowing and Ring Room Operatives was formed in 1886, following a strike at Oldham during the previous year. Predominantly for unskilled female workers, including ring spinners, it nevertheless contained the more skilled strippers and grinders, men who maintained the carding engines. They gained control of the union, enhancing their skilled status and earnings by restricting entry to the trade and by limiting the number of men per machine.[63]

References

1. The raw cotton figures used here are in B. R. Mitchell, *British Historical Statistics* (Cambridge University Press, 1988), p. 332 and P. Deane & W. A. Cole, *British Economic Growth, 1688–1959* (Cambridge University Press, 1962), p. 187.

2. D. Farnie, *The English Cotton Industry and the World Market, 1815–1896* (Clarendon Press, 1979), pp. 7–8 & 24.

3. T. Ellison, *The Cotton Trade of Great Britain* (1886, reprinted Frank Cass, 1968), pp. 106–9.

4. R. Robson, *The Cotton Industry in Britain* (Macmillan, 1957), pp. 4–5 & 338.

5. The literature on the cotton famine is considerable, but useful accounts are to be found in J. K. Walton, *Lancashire: A Social History, 1558–1939* (Manchester University Press, 1987), pp. 284–6; C. B. Phillips and J. H. Smith, *Lancashire and Cheshire from AD 1540* (Longman, 1994), pp. 248–52; and, especially, Farnie, *Cotton Industry*, pp. 135–70.

6. W. Farrer & J. Brownbill (eds), *A History of the County of Lancaster*, Pt 13 (London, 1920), p. 382.

7. Farnie, *Cotton Industry*, ch. 2; S. Pollard, *Peaceful Conquest* (Oxford University Press, 1981), pp. 18–19.

8. T. H. Freeman, H. B. Rogers & R. H. Kinvig, *Lancashire, Cheshire & the Isle of Man* (Thomas Nelson, 1966), pp. 95–9.

9. J. D. Marshall, 'Colonisation as a Factor in the Planting of Towns in North-West England', in H. J. Dyos (ed.), *The Study of Urban History* (Edward Arnold, 1968), pp. 215–30.

10. C. H. Lee, 'The Cotton Textile Industry' in R. Church (ed.), *The Dynamics of the Industrial Revolution* (George Allen and Unwin, 1980), p. 176.

11. Farnie, *Cotton Industry*, pp. 301–12; Walton, *Lancashire*, pp. 199–200; Farrer & Brownbill, *History*, p. 391.

12. Farnie, *Cotton Industry*, pp. 215 & 286.

13. Ellison, *Cotton Trade*, pp. 133–40; Farnie, *Cotton Industry*, chs. 6 & 7.

14. P. L. Payne, *British Entrepreneurship in the Nineteenth Century* (Macmillan, 1988), pp. 14–20; L. Hannah, 'Mergers in British Manufacturing Industry, 1880–1918', *Oxford Economic Papers*, (1974), pp. 1–20; P. L. Cook, 'The Calico Printing Industry', in P. L. Cook, *Effects of Mergers* (Allen & Unwin, 1958), ch. 2; Farrer & Brownbill, *History*, pp. 392, 397, & 399; J. Singleton, *Lancashire on the Scrapheap* (Pasold, 1991), pp. 8–9; G. C. Allen, *British Industries and Their Organisation* (Longman, 1970), p. 243.

15. Farnie, *Cotton Industry*, pp. 213–15.

16. O. Ashmore, *Industrial Archaeology of Lancashire* (David and Charles, 1969), pp. 49–51.

17. Farnie, *Cotton Trade*, pp. 209–11.

18. Farnie, *Cotton Trade*, pp. 315–18; J. S. Lyons, 'Vertical Integration in the British Cotton Industry, 1825–1850: A Revision', *Journal of Economic History*, 45 (1985), pp. 419–25.

19. Lee, 'Textile Industry', pp. 162–80.

20. R. Marsden, *Cotton Weaving: Its Development, Principles, and Practice* (London, 1895), p. 95.

21. G. Timmins, *The Last Shift* (Manchester University Press, 1993), pp. 19–23.

22. T. W. Fox, *The Mechanism of Weaving* (Macmillan, 1922), pp. 580–9; Farnie, *Cotton Industry*, pp. 306–7; Ashmore, *Industrial Archaeology*, pp. 51–2.

23. Timmins, *Last Shift*, pp. 110–11.

24. Timmins, *Last Shift*, ch. 7.

25. Timmins, *Last Shift*, pp. 158–9.

26. Farnie, *Cotton Industry*, pp. 198–9 & 282.

27. R. Boyson, *The Ashworth Enterprise* (Clarendon Press, 1970), p. 75.

28. Farnie, *Cotton Industry*, p. 199.

29. R. Bracegirdle, 'Textile Finishing in the North West', in J. H. Smith (ed.), *The Great Human Exploit* (Phillimore, 1973), pp. 38–9.

30. *Census of England and Wales, 1911: Occupations and Industries*, vol. X, Pt 1 (1913), p. 7.

31. Deane & Cole, *Economic Growth*, p. 190.

32. W. Mass and W. Lazonick, 'The British Cotton Industry and International Competitive Advantage: the State of the Debates', *Business History*, 32 (1990), pp. 11–13.

33. Farnie, *Cotton Trade*, pp. 215–40.

34. This is evident from the map and discussion in Freeman, Rodgers and Kinvig, *Lancashire*, pp. 85–9.

35. A. Kidd, *Manchester* (Ryburn, 1993), pp. 106–8.

36. Farrer & Brownbill, *History*, p. 392; Phillips & Smith, *Lancashire*, pp. 240–5.

37. Mass & Lazonick, 'British Cotton', pp. 13–14; Walton, *Lancashire*, pp. 206–7.

38. Farnie, *Cotton Trade*, p. 7.

39. Deane & Cole, *Economic Growth*, p. 187.

40. Farnie, *Cotton Trade*, pp. 90–3.

41. Farnie, *Cotton Trade*, pp. 91 & 96–119; S. Chapman, *Merchant Enterprise in Britain*, (Cambridge University Press, 1993), ch. 4.

42. However, the absolute figure rose from 4,410 million square yards (3,687 million square metres) to 6,650 million square yards (5,560 million square metres) during this period. See Robson, *Cotton Industry*, p. 4.

43. R. E. Tyson, 'The Cotton Industry' in D. H. Aldcroft, *The Development of British Industry and Foreign Competition, 1875–1914* (Allen & Unwin, 1968), pp. 104–8; Robson, *Cotton Industry*, p. 3.

44. For a succinct discussion of the entrepreneurial failure issue see Payne, *Entrepreneurship*, pp. 43–7.

45. For a summary of historians' charges against cotton entrepreneurs, see L. G. Sandberg, *Lancashire in Decline* (Ohio State University, 1774), pp. 8–10 & 93–5.

46. L. G. Sandberg, 'American Rings and English Mules: The Role of Economic Rationality', in S. B. Saul, *Technological Change: The United States and Britain in the 19th Century* (Methuen, 1970), pp. 120–40; W. Lazonick, 'Factor Costs and the Diffusion of Ring Spinning in Britain Prior to World War I', *The Quarterly Journal of Economics*, 96 (1981), pp. 89–109; Mass and Lazonick, 'British Cotton', pp. 24–7.

47. For summary comment on the former issue, see Mass & Lazonick, 'British Cotton', p. 28 and on the latter issue, see G. Saxonhouse and G. Wright, 'Stubborn mules and vertical integration: the disappearing constraint?', *Economic History Review*, 40 (1987), pp. 87–94 and D. M. Higgins, 'Rings, mules and structural constraints in the Lancashire textile industry, c.1945–c.1965', *Economic History Review*, 46 (1993), pp. 342–62.

48. Mass and Lazonick, 'British Cotton', pp. 10–36.

49. E. Hopwood, *A History of the Lancashire Cotton Industry and the Amalgamated Weavers' Association* (Manchester, 1969), p. 65; A. Fowler & T. Wyke, *The Barefoot Aristocrats* (Kelsall, 1987), pp. 44–5.

50. Fowler & Wyke, *Aristocrats*, pp. 49–51. The Preston Strike is analysed in H. I. Dutton & J. King, *Ten Per Cent and No Surrender* (Cambridge University Press, 1981).

51. Hopwood, *Lancashire Cotton*, pp. 33–6; H. A. Turner, *Trade Union Growth, Structure and Policy* (Allen & Unwin, 1962), pp. 128–35; A. Bullen, 'Pragmatism vs. Principle: Cotton Employers and the Origins of an Industrial Relations System' in J. A. Jowitt & A. J. McIvor, (eds), *Employers & Labour in the English Textile Industries, 1850–1939* (Routledge, 1988), pp. 30–4.

52. Fowler & Wyke, *Aristocrats*, pp. 48–9.

53. S. J. Chapman, *The Lancashire Cotton Industry* (Manchester University Press, 1904), p. 237. For an account of one major strike see J. E. King, '"We Could Eat the Police!": Popular Violence in the North Lancashire Cotton Strike of 1878', *Victorian Studies*, 28 (1985), pp. 439–71.

54. Bullen, 'Pragmatism', pp. 34–7.

55. Tyson, 'Cotton Industry', pp. 101–2.

56. A. McIvor, 'Cotton Employers' Organisations and Labour Relations', in

Jowitt & McIvor, *Employers & Labour*, pp. 6–7 & 9; Lazonick, 'Cotton Industry', pp. 25–6.

57. McIvor, 'Employers', pp. 2–5.

58. Hopwood, *Lancashire Cotton*, pp. 47–8 & 53–6; A. Bullen, *The Lancashire Weavers' Union* (Amalgamated Textile Weavers' Union, 1984), ch. 2.

59. For discussion on this point, see W. Lazonick. 'Production Relations, Labor Productivity, and the Choice of Technique: British and US Cotton Spinning', *Journal of Economic History*, 41 (1981), esp. pp. 501–3 & 514–15.

60. Fowler & Wyke, *Aristocrats*, ch. 6; R. Penn, 'Trade Union Organisation and Skill in the Cotton and Engineering Industries in Britain, 1850–1960', *Social History*, 8 (1983), pp. 39–40; Walton, *Lancashire*, pp. 266–7; Hopwood, *Lancashire Cotton*, pp. 57–8.

61. Lazonick, 'Cotton Industry', p. 26; Singleton, *Scrapheap*, pp. 9–10; Lazonick, 'Production Relations', pp. 503–10.

62. Penn, 'Union Organisation', pp. 43–4; Walton, *Lancashire*, pp. 267–8; Turner, *Union Growth*, pp. 128 & 153–63; Hopwood, *Lancashire Cotton*, pp. 59–62 & 68–73; Bullen, *Lancashire Weavers*, ch. 3.

63. Turner, *Union Growth*, pp. 144–7 & 163–7; A. Bullen & A. Fowler, *The Cardroom Workers' Union* (The Amalgamated Textile Workers' Union, 1986), chs 2 & 3.

CHAPTER FOUR

The Cotton Industry in Decline

1914 AND BEYOND

Falling output: World War I and the inter-war period

he First World War brought severe difficulties for the Lancashire cotton industry. At an early stage, manpower requirements of the armed forces led to labour shortages, though these proved to be temporary. In part, this was because more women and girls were employed. But it was also because, with restricted shipping space, raw cotton supplies became scarcer and, from 1917, they were allocated to firms by a Cotton Control Board composed of representatives from unions, employers and the government. Inevitably, cotton production was much reduced, which, coupled with shipping difficulties and keen competition from overseas producers, caused cloth exports to drop sharply.[1] Indeed, the record export figure of 6,469 million linear metres attained by Britain's cotton producers in 1913 was virtually halved by the time hostilities ceased.[2]

During the immediate post-war years, the industry appeared to make a remarkable recovery. Prices and profits rose sharply, with both overseas and domestic customers eagerly purchasing the cotton goods that wartime had denied them. Shareholders earned far higher dividends, payments to those in the spinning trade averaging no less than 40 per cent in 1920. Greater borrowing was also encouraged, the loans being partly used to purchase new machinery. But they also financed take-over bids at unrealistically high prices, speculators being attracted by the promise of a continuing revival in the industry's fortunes. All too soon, however, the abnormal demand for cotton goods was satisfied and in 1921 the boom collapsed, leaving firms with the problem of meeting heavy interest charges as their profitability declined. Dividend levels and investment expenditure suffered accordingly.[3]

Throughout the inter-war years, as the trend in export sales remained downwards, the industry operated at a much-reduced level. Thus, between 1913 and 1937, cotton cloth output declined by more than half, from 7,360 to 3,328 million linear metres. Yarn production fared little better, the decrease during these years being from 872 to 616 thousand tonnes, virtually a third. The differing experience of the two sectors reflects a less dramatic fall in yarn than in cloth exports, as well as a rise in yarn sales to the hosiery industry.[4] And some firms protected themselves from falling exports by switching partly to cotton and rayon (artificial silk) mixtures or entirely to rayon.[5]

Falling output: World War II and the post-war years

The outbreak of World War II brought further problems for the industry. In 1941, it was included amongst the Government's 'concentration' schemes, which aimed to minimise the resources used by less-essential industries, without destroying their markets. As far as cotton production was concerned, there was a need to save shipping space by restricting raw cotton imports, to release labour for the armed forces and to provide wartime storage space in cotton warehouses and factories in a part of the country that was deemed relatively safe from aerial attack. Once more, a Cotton Board was established to assist the industry.[6]

In the event, raw cotton imports fell back each year between 1940 and 1945 to only around half their pre-war levels. Meanwhile, labour shortages quickly emerged and to prevent further losses, the cotton trades were designated amongst the 'essential work' industries in January 1942. Largely as a result of these developments, the output of cotton yarn and cloth continued its inter-war decline, falling to around half pre-war levels by 1945.[7]

During the immediate post-war years, the industry showed a modest recovery, output of cotton cloth rising from 1,520 million linear metres in 1946 to a peak of 2,098 million linear metres in 1951.[8] Export sales were particularly influential here, as the German and Japanese cotton industries needed time to re-establish themselves. Due to low wages and poor working conditions, labour proved difficult to attract, and this held back the rate at which the industry grew. Moreover, raw cotton prices were relatively high for Lancashire spinners. This was because America and other countries sold the raw cotton they grew far more cheaply at home than overseas.[9]

Since the early 1950s, the downward trend in cotton production has been virtually unrelenting, as FIGURE 12 reveals.[10] Both cloth and yarn output fell substantially each decade, with the

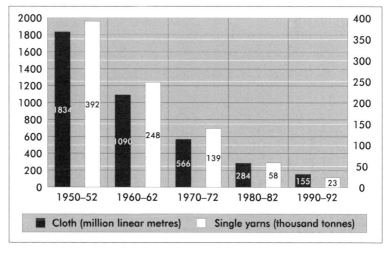

FIGURE 12a.
UK cloth and yarn output: cotton.

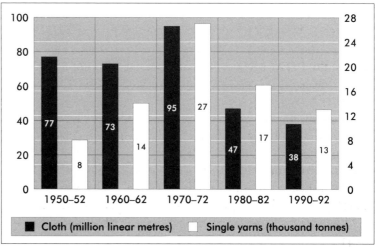

FIGURE 12b.
UK cloth and yarn output: cotton/man-made fibre mixtures.

former reducing by 92 per cent over the period as a whole and the latter by 94 per cent. Production of cloth and yarn made from man-made fibre and cotton mixtures fared rather better, though this, too, declined sharply during the 1970s and 1980s. By then, indeed, Lancashire's diminishing number of cotton mills were turning increasingly to the manufacture of man-made fibre products, many abandoning cotton production altogether.

Impact of overseas competiton

The danger to the cotton industry in depending so highly on overseas markets during its peak years was revealed when the massive export losses incurred during World War I proved to be permanent. It is true that, although much reduced from their pre-war levels, exports of both cloth and yarn held up fairly well until the late 1920s. But, thereafter, except for a temporary respite after World War II, the trend was relentlessly downwards, especially in lower-grade goods. Thus, whereas exports of cotton piece-goods, measured in linear metres, averaged 3,634 million from 1927–9, they fell to 875 million at the peak of the post-war recovery in 1949 and to as little as 146 million from 1978–80. This was a mere 2 per cent of the 1913 total.[11]

The fall in overseas sales plainly accounts for much of the cotton industry's long-term decline. The problem arose partly because other countries, especially in Asia, continued to expand their own cotton industries, so they required smaller quantities of yarn and cloth from Britain. But the situation was exacerbated as several of these countries, led by Japan, increasingly invaded Britain's traditional export markets.

The early impact of these developments is only too evident in the case of the crucial Indian market. Here, cotton piece-goods woven in mills rose from an annual average of 1,141 million linear yards (1,043 million linear metres) in 1909–13 to one of 4,101 million linear yards (3,750 million linear metres) in 1937–8. During the same period, total imports of cotton piece goods into the country fell almost 75 per cent from 2,741 to 706 million linear yards (2,506 to 646 million linear metres) and those from the United Kingdom nearly 90 per cent from 2,669 to 291 million linear yards (2,441 to 266 million linear metres). Japanese cotton producers, meanwhile, were able to raise their Indian sales from 4 to 441 million linear yards (3.7 to 403 million linear metres).[12]

Other influences on the loss of Lancashire's cotton export markets during the inter-war years can also be identified, amongst them an overvalued currency. This occurred between 1925 and 1931, as Britain returned to the gold standard with sterling exchanging at too high a rate against the dollar. As a result, the price of British exports rose, making them less competitive in international markets.[13] Also taking its toll was the widespread introduction of tariffs to protect local cotton industries. That in India had reached no less than 25 per cent by 1931, its impact being strengthened by the efforts of Gandhi and the Congress Party to boycott imported cottons.[14]

It has also been argued that the comparative advantages Britain had gained in cotton production before World War I were lost to other countries, especially Japan, during the inter-war years. Thus, not only did these countries benefit from lower labour costs, but also from investment in improved machinery. In Japan, this included the highly-efficient Toyoda automatic loom, along with machines for blending raw cotton, so that cheaper, short-staple fibres could be used with ring-frames. As a result, remarkable increases were obtained in output per worker, that in spinning rising by 63 per cent between 1926 and 1935 and that in weaving by 122 per cent.[15] Additionally, Japanese cotton producers created a highly efficient marketing system, making use of trained Japanese staff, and invested heavily in management training, helping the leading firms to co-ordinate activity effectively as the number of mills they operated increased.[16]

During World War II, Britain's cotton exports continued to fall, as production was curtailed. However, they recovered steadily during the latter half of the 1940s, though not rapidly enough to prevent other countries from starting their own cotton industries. They included Australia, South Africa and Southern Rhodesia (Zimbabwe), countries which, in the early 1930s, had made trade agreements allowing British cottons to be imported at preferential rates of duty.[17]

But it was not only with the loss of further overseas markets that Lancashire's cotton producers had to contend in the early post-war years. Increasingly, though by no means rapidly, cloth from Europe and Asia was imported into Britain, as home producers were unable to meet consumers' needs. The situation was worsened by a dollar shortage, which curtailed purchases of raw cotton from the United States, by the need to bolster exports of cotton goods to help pay for essential imports of fuel, food and raw materials and by the abolition of clothes rationing in 1949, which stimulated home demand for cotton goods.[18] Between 1936 and 1938, annual cotton cloth imports into Britain averaged 41 million square metres, a figure that had risen to 282 million between 1949 and 1951.[19]

During subsequent decades, cotton import penetration continued apace, amidst sustained demands for controls to be implemented. In his annual report for 1957, the chairman of the Lancashire Cotton Corporation (a company formed in 1929 to amalgamate coarse spinning capacity) noted with concern that, for the first time in two centuries, imports of cotton cloth into the United Kingdom exceeded exports.[20] And, with more than a hint of desperation, the general secretary of the spinners' union reflected that it was hard to imagine how the government could not be persuaded that the industry was 'being bled to death'.[21] By this time, Japan's lead in the trade had been relinquished to India and Hong Kong, though Pakistan and China were also making notable inroads, particularly with grey (unbleached) cotton cloths. By 1984, India supplied 23 per cent of the United Kingdom's imports of this product, Pakistan 13 per cent and China and Hong Kong 10 per cent each. But the EEC countries, led by West Germany, were also prominent in the trade, supplying a further 17 per cent of the total. During the following year, Britain's total trade deficit in cotton and man-made fibre cloths (bleached, dyed and printed) reached no less than a billion square metres.[22]

Responding to decline: import controls

At an early stage in the cotton industry's decline, the issue arose of reducing overseas competition by controlling yarn and cloth imports. Indeed, it became embroiled in a long-running and wider debate about the return to tariff protection for British industry. This culminated in the 1932 Import Duties Act, passed in the wake of the Wall Street Crash and the ensuing slump in world trade and production. The Act, from which Commonwealth goods were exempted, imposed an import duty of 10 per cent on cotton yarn and 20 per cent on cotton cloth, bringing an immediate fall in cotton imports which, though small, had been rising. It may be noted, too, that the introduction of the 1932 Ottawa Agreements, which fixed levels of preferential tariffs for Britain within the Commonwealth, helped to increase Britain's cotton exports to the Dominions and Colonies.[23]

Preferential tariffs, however, did not bring any marked long-term benefits to the Lancashire cotton industry. This was largely because imports of cotton goods from the Indian sub-continent and from Hong Kong were allowed to enter Britain without paying duty. And as the level of these imports grew rapidly during the post-war years, Lancashire's cotton interest pressed vociferously for curbs to be imposed. Amongst the arguments they used was that Chinese imports were being sold at 'political prices', which were 'unrelated to the costs of production'.[24]

In 1958, as a general election loomed, the British government finally took action, negotiating voluntary quotas for grey cloth imports from India, Pakistan and Hong Kong. However, since these were set higher than the prevailing level of imports from these countries, they scarcely resolved the problem.[25] During the early 1960s, they were supplemented with bilateral agreements limiting cloth imports from non-Commonwealth countries, including Japan and China. At the same time, member countries of GATT (General Agreement on Tariffs and Trade) – an organisation formed in 1948 to lower international trade barriers – formulated rules by which quota agreements on cloth imports from low-wage countries were to be based. These operated in favour of the developed countries, so as to ease their adjustment to cheap imports, even though this was scarcely in line with GATT principles. They also formed the model for later bilateral negotiations made under the provision of the MFA (Multi-Fibre Agreement), which was introduced in 1974 and which was to remain in force until the end of 1992.[26]

Responding to decline: changes in the industry

During the inter-war years, as demand for Lancashire cottons fell and as small-scale family firms persisted, various attempts were made to reduce competition in the industry.[27] Both price fixing and quota schemes were planned, a key aim being to prevent some firms from extending their sales at the expense of others by means of 'weak selling' – charging prices for yarn and cloth that were less than the cost of production. The most comprehensive of these schemes received statutory approval by means of the 1939 Cotton Industry (Reorganisation) Act, amongst the provisions of which were minimum price schemes for the industry.[28] However, with the outbreak of war, the situation changed. The reduced output of cotton goods made price rises more likely than price reductions and statutory price controls were introduced.[29]

The abandonment of these controls in the late 1940s, coupled with the revival of imported textiles, prompted the industry to develop further price and quota schemes. These proved difficult to establish in the weaving branch, however, given the large number of small-scale producers. Moreover, those that were successfully established in the spinning and finishing branches eventually fell foul of monopolies and restrictive practice legislation. Thus, the Monopolies Commission forced the Federation of Calico Printers to abandon their minimum price and quota scheme in 1954, on the grounds that it kept prices for their products artificially high. A similar fate befell the price maintenance scheme devised by the Yarn Spinners' Association. This came before the Restrictive Practices Court in 1958 and was rejected on the grounds that it did not give substantial benefit to the public.[30]

Abandonment of price and quota agreements, along with the continuing fall in cotton exports, paved the way for an alternative means of controlling competition between domestic producers. This was to promote mergers in the industry, a policy which had been applied with limited success during the inter-war years.[31] It was re-introduced during the 1960s, the initiative being taken by the man-made fibre producers. Courtaulds, the largest concern amongst them, led the way, prompted by the fear that the continued decline of cotton production would threaten their sales of rayon fibres to Lancashire spinners. They reasoned that Lancashire cotton firms would need to diversify into man-made fibres if they were to survive. And this could be best achieved by the formation of large companies, which would introduce fresh management, keep prices stable and eliminate excess capacity. Furthermore, large textile producers would have greater bargaining power in relation to the major retail chains they supplied.[32]

The take-overs began in earnest during 1963. Courtaulds bought directly, but ICI, also a major supplier of man-made fibres to Lancashire firms, preferred to fund intermediaries, particularly Viyella International and Carrington and Dewhurst, to act on their behalf. By 1966, these three concerns, along with English Sewing Cotton, effectively controlled the Lancashire cotton industry. Courtaulds alone possessed 30 per cent of spindles and 20 per cent of looms in 1968.[33]

One result of the merger boom was to create a much higher degree of vertical integration (firms undertaking successive stages of production) despite the survival of numerous small, specialist concerns, particularly in weaving. As a rule, the leading firms integrated forwards, albeit to varying degrees, into spinning, knitting, weaving, finishing and making up. That they adopted several new product areas reflects a desire to safeguard their markets, though Courtaulds did not apparently set out to achieve a high degree of vertical integration.[34]

In addition to controlling competition, the problem of dealing with excess capacity in the industry had to be faced. Prior to the mid-1930s, a considerable quantity of redundant looms and spindles had been scrapped as firms reduced capacity or went out of business. However, the process was facilitated by the establishment of the Spindles Board under the provisions of the Cotton Spinning Industry Act, 1936. The Board's purpose was to buy and scrap cotton spinning machinery and mills. It could borrow up to £2 million, the interest and capital being financed by a levy on all cotton spinners. During the three years the board existed, it acquired and destroyed some 6 million spindles, about 13 per cent of the 1936 total. In consequence, numerous mills were closed.[35]

A further scheme for reducing excess capacity was introduced by the 1959 Cotton Industry Act. The aim was to reduce capacity by at least 50 per cent in spinning and 40 per cent in weaving and finishing. Again, a levy was imposed on the industry, but this time it amounted to only a third of the total required, the other two-thirds coming from the Treasury. The scheme lasted five years, resulting in spindle numbers being halved, looms being reduced by a quarter and over 200 firms giving up production altogether[36] (PLATE 22).

The 1959 Act also implemented another strategy to deal with the cotton industry's decline. This was re-equipping with up-to-date machinery. The matter had previously been tackled by central

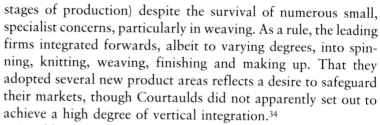

PLATE 22. Demolition of the chimney at Stocks Bridge Mill, Preston, 1992. As cotton firms went out of business, the mills they vacated proved suitable for a variety of uses. Even so, a high proportion have been demolished, including examples of architectural distinction.

government with the passage of the 1948 Cotton Spinning (Re-equipment Subsidy) Act, which gave 25 per cent re-equipment subsidies in the spinning branch. However, this was unpopular both with employers, because it required them to amalgamate or work closely as groups, and with unions, because it imposed shift working. With or without the subsidy, though, the spinners made some progress with re-investment during the 1950s. Thus, the number of ring spindles rose from 5.64 million in 1946 to 7.49 million in 1958, a rise of nearly one-third. By then, the number of ring spindles exceeded the number of mule spindles.[37] In the weaving branch, however, much slower progress occurred, automatic looms making up only 14 per cent of the 1958 total. The rising price of machinery, which more than doubled during the 1950s, the under-utilisation of existing equipment and the limited profitability of cotton firms in the face of powerful overseas competition, were key factors in limiting investment levels.[38]

The 1959 Act played a major role in this modernisation programme because part of the funds it made available could be used for purchasing new machinery. In the event, though, cotton firms remained reluctant to invest, the chairman of the Lancashire Cotton Corporation wondering in his 1960 report whether it was worthwhile to do so as cotton imports continued to rise.[39] Accordingly, progress was extremely modest. from 1960–5, only about 0.7 million spindles and 11,000 looms were installed under the provisions of the Act; in neither case was this more than a small proportion of total capacity.[40] Since then, the more successful firms have innovated further, not least with regard to shuttleless looms, which use jets of air or small projectiles to propel the weft through the warps (PLATE 23). By 1980, 22 per cent of British looms were

PLATE 23a (below) and 23b (opposite). Shuttleless looms. The photograph shows examples used by Hilden Manufacturing Company of Oswaldtwistle. That weaving striped fabric is a projectile loom dating from about 1980, coupled to a mechanical Jacquard. It can insert 230 picks (lengths of weft thread) per minute.

(Author's photograph)

PLATE 23b.
This Sulzer Ruti
loom, also at
Hilden's dates from
1995 and is linked to
an electronic Jac-
quard. It can insert
an astonishing 600
picks per minute.
(The plain looms it
replaced ran at no
more than 150 picks
per minute.)

shuttleless, a figure few other countries could exceed. Investment in these looms seems to have been favoured by the vertically-integrated firms that emerged during the 1960s, not least because they could ensure a more stable market through their control of subsequent production stages.[41]

Investment in up-to-date machinery was associated with the construction of several new 'supermills' – including that at Skelmersdale – during the late 1960s and 1970s.[42] However, these did not produce efficiently enough to meet the competition from low-cost imports. In the event, a more successful strategy was to diversify into the production of specialist, high-quality products, perhaps using artificial fibres. For example, the Amalgamated Cotton Mills Trust, Ltd reported in 1958 that its Chorley factory was making 'Aertex', a knitted synthetic cloth, which was much in demand for underwear.[43]

The labour force

With the end of the post-World War I boom, and the permanent reduction of output in their industry, Lancashire's cotton operatives entered a period when short-time working, cuts in wage rates and lower levels of employment became all too common. Thus, between 1926 and 1939, the labour force in the UK cotton industry was reduced by 34 per cent from 575,000 to 378,000, whilst unemployment levels in the industry remained stubbornly above 10 per cent, reaching the dreadful level of 43 per cent in 1931.[44] As to wages, weavers earning around £3 in

1920 were paid less than £2 in 1937, whilst spinners earning around £5 in 1920 found their income reduced to £3 10s (£3.50) in 1932. Probably, therefore, spinners no longer earned more than the average for craftsmen and weavers received less than general labourers.[45]

This type of evidence hints at the high levels of distress that beset so many Lancashire cotton workers during the inter-war years. Generalisations are hard to make, but some groups and some districts were more badly hit than others, though there was much variation within them, whilst the intensity of suffering inevitably depended on trade cycle movements. The indications are, however, that the weaving districts of north-east Lancashire were worse hit than the spinning districts further south, though, in both areas, firms producing fine, high-quality goods, including the Nelson weavers, were better placed.[46]

Faced with these difficulties, the cotton trade unions, especially the weavers, took a militant stance. Two major waves of unrest occurred. One was in 1918–19, when the first general strike of cotton operatives took place. With high profits being earned, they managed to secure wage increases and a reduction in working hours to 48 per week. The latter objective had long been sought, one effect being to end the 6 a.m. start to the working day. The wage increases proved short-lived, however, employers combining effectively to impose cuts in 1922 after the post-war boom collapsed.

The other major period of labour unrest was in 1929–32. It occurred against a background of deepening economic depression and of hardening attitudes amongst cotton employers with regard to trade union activities. Two matters were in particular dispute. One was the imposition of further wage cuts, which were more severe than those in other industries. The other was the employers' attempt to raise the number of looms per weaver to six or eight – the 'more-looms' system. The weavers took strike action against working eight looms and though they achieved their aim, they were compelled to sign the Midland Agreement. This set lower piece rates for more-loom weavers than for the standard four-loom weavers, enabling the former to earn only slightly higher wages than the latter, despite their greater productivity.[47]

The outbreak of war in 1939 quickly turned the labour surplus in the Lancashire cotton industry into a shortage, not only because of enlistment in the forces, but also because other work, including that in munitions factories, paid higher wages and offered better working conditions. Moreover, the average age of cotton workers was relatively high, having reached 37 years by the end of the war, compared with 34 years in 1931 and 29 years in 1911. This gave rise to high retirement rates. Between 1937 and 1945, employment in the industry dropped by 42 per cent and it was estimated that over 160,000 additional workers would be needed to operate at the pre-war level again.[48]

During the immediate post-war years, a range of measures was introduced in an attempt to overcome the industry's labour shortages. Some, including the abandonment of mule spinners' control over piecers' wages, arose from recommendations made by the Evershed Committee, which reported in October, 1945. They proved inadequate, though, and as the need to earn overseas currency to pay for imports became more pressing, other expedients were tried. Amongst them was the introduction of part-time evening shifts for married women, many of whom were experienced in the cotton industry, but had stopped work when the war ended. Foreign labour was also employed, especially European Voluntary Workers, who were mostly homeless people from countries in central and eastern parts of the Continent. The first group, comprising twenty Polish females, arrived at the start of 1947 and numbers swelled to around 17,000 by May, 1950.[49] Immigrant workers thus made a notable, but as yet undetermined, contribution to meeting labour needs in the cotton industry and continued to do so in later decades.

During the 1950s and 1960s, more workers left the cotton industry as further contraction in output occurred. As a result, labour shortages were still encountered, especially during trade upturns. For example, the Lancashire Cotton Corporation was 700 operatives short in 1960, despite granting a wage increase of 7.5 per cent, along with shorter working hours and improved working conditions.[50] Throughout this period, however, the wage increases of cotton workers were lower than those of other groups. With generally high levels of employment, alternative work was as a rule easier to find than during the inter-war years[51] and than they would be in the 1970s and 1980s.

As well as dealing with labour shortages, attempts were made to use workers more efficiently. In particular, cotton unions were persuaded to extend shift-working systems, to which they had been traditionally opposed. This was an important development in an industry which was becoming more capital-intensive and which, in consequence, needed to use machinery as fully as possible in order to minimise capital costs per unit of output. By the mid-1950s, the introduction of two shifts per day had become common and by 1963, the Lancashire Cotton Corporation could report that half the yarn it produced came from machinery operating on more than one shift.[52] Meanwhile, as union opposition weakened, night-shift working began to make headway. Yet the prohibition on night work for women limited the extent to which it could be implemented. To compensate for the more unsocial hours that shift working entailed, the unions secured shorter working hours and higher wage rates.

A further attempt to improve labour efficiency must also be noted. This was the replacement of the industry's traditional uniform wage lists by wage lists giving accurate measures of workloads. These helped to increase labour productivity, with, for example, the proportion of weavers operating more than four looms rising from a third to a half between 1948 and 1955. The new wage lists also helped to reduce wage costs per unit of output, though not to the levels achieved in competitor countries.[53]

References

1. G. C. Allen, *British Industries and their Organisation* (Longman, 1970 edition), pp. 229–30; J. K. Walton, *Lancashire: A Social History, 1558–1939* (Manchester University Press, 1989), p. 326.

2. B. R. Mitchell, *British Historical Statistics* (Cambridge University Press, 1988), pp. 356–7.

3. R. Robson, *The Cotton Industry in Britain* (Macmillan, 1957) p. 7; Walton, *Lancashire*, pp. 328–9; A. Fowler & T. Wyke, *The Barefoot Aristocrats* (Kelsall, 1987), p. 145: W. Lazonick, 'The Cotton Industry' in B. Elbaum & W. Lazonick, *The Decline of the British Economy* (Clarendon Press, 1986), p. 31.

4. Mitchell, *Historical Statistics*, pp. 355 & 357.

5. J. Singleton, *Lancashire on the Scrapheap* (Pasold, 1991) p. 11.

6. Robson, *Cotton Industry*, pp. 12–13; Allen, *Industries*, pp. 235–6. For consideration of the Cotton Board's work, see M. W. Dupree, 'Struggling with Destiny: the Cotton Industry, Overseas Trade Policy and the Cotton Board, 1940–1959', *Business History*, 32 (1990), pp. 107–25.

7. Robson, *Cotton Industry*, pp. 13–16.

8. Mitchell, *Historical Statistics*, p. 355.

9. Robson, *Cotton Industry*, p. 16.

10. The figures are derived from the Central Statistical Office's *Annual Abstract of Statistics* series.

11. Mitchell, *Historical Statistics*, p. 357; Allen, *Industries*, p. 232.

12. Robson, *Cotton Industry*, p. 10.

13. S. Pollard, *The Development of the British Economy, 1914–1967* (Edward Arnold, 1969), pp. 216–23.

14. Robson, Cotton Industry, p. 10.

15. Allen, *Industries*, p. 234.

16. W. Mass and W. Lazonick, 'The British Cotton Industry and International Comparative Advantage: the State of the Debates', *Business History*, 32, (1990) pp. 37–50.

17. Robson, *Cotton Industry*, p. 14.

18. Pollard, *British Economy*, pp. 356–8; Robson, *Cotton Industry*, p. 15.

19. Robson, *Cotton Industry*, p. 15.

20. Reported in *The Manchester Guardian*, 31.12.1957.

21. Amalgamated Association of Operative Cotton Spinners & Twiners, *Quarterly Report*, December 1957, p. 6.

22. Amalgamated Association of Operative Cotton Spinners & Twiners, *Quarterly Report*, October 1957; *Partnership for Profit: A Study into Relationships between Textile Manufacturers and Merchant Converters* (National Economic Development Office, 1986), pp. 5 & 52.

23. Robson, *Cotton Industry*, p. 9; A. E. Musson, *The Growth of British Industry* (Batsford, 1978), pp. 268–320.

24. Lancashire Cotton Corporation, *Annual Report for 1957*, reported in *The Manchester Guardian*, 31.12.1957.

25. Dupree, 'Cotton Board', pp. 121–5; Fowler & Wyke, *Aristocrats*, p. 206.

26. 'World Textiles', *Financial Times*, 3.10.1991.

27. On the persistence of family firms, see Lazonick, 'Cotton Industry', pp. 44–5.

28. Robson, *Cotton Industry*, pp. 16–17; Singleton, *Scrapheap*, p. 17; Allen, *British Industries*, p. 247.

29. Singleton, *Scrapheap*, p. 28.

30. Singleton, *Scrapheap*, ch. 9.

31. For details, see Musson, *British Industry*, pp. 320–1; Singleton, *Scrapheap*, pp. 14–15; Lazonick, 'Cotton Industry', pp. 32–3; and M. W. Kirby, 'The Lancashire Cotton Industry in the Inter-War Years: A Study in Organisational Change', *Business History*, 16 (1974), pp. 149–52.

32. Singleton, *Scrapheap*, pp. 218–19.

33. Allen, *British Industries*, p. 258; Singleton, *Scrapheap*, pp. 219–30.

34. Singleton, *Scrapheap*, pp. 222–3; Allen, *British Industries*, p. 259; Lazonick, 'Cotton Industry', pp. 37–9.

35. Singleton, *Scrapheap*, pp. 12–14; Allen, *British Industries*, p. 247.

36. Singleton, *Scrapheap*, pp. 154–67; Allen, *British Industries*, pp. 257–8.

37. Singleton, *Scrapheap*, pp. 34–5.

38. Singleton, *Scrapheap*, pp. 5 & 7.

39. Reported in *The Guardian*, 17.1.1961.

40. Allen, *British Industries*, p. 258.

41. Singleton, *Scrapheap*, pp. 162–7.

42. European Commission, *Panorama of EU Industry 94*, (EC Publications, 1994), pp. 14–15.

43. 1957 Annual General Meeting of the Company, reported in *The Guardian*, 22.2.1958; C. B. Phillips & J. H. Smith, *Lancashire and Cheshire From AD 1540* (Longman, 1994), p. 324.

44. Singleton, *Scrapheap*, pp. 11–12; Phillips & Smith, *Lancashire and Cheshire*, p. 322.

45. A. Fowler, 'Lancashire Cotton Trade Unionism in the Inter-War Years' in J. A. Jowitt & A. J. McIvor (eds), *Employers and Labour in the English Textile Industries, 1850–1939* (Routledge, 1988), p. 122

46. Walton, *Lancashire*, p. 339; Allen, *British Industries*, p. 235; Fowler, 'Trade Unionism', pp. 116–17.

47. Fowler, 'Trade Unionism', pp. 113–23; A. J. McIvor, 'Cotton Employers' Organisations and Labour Relations, 1890–1939', in Jowitt & McIvor, *Employers and Labour*, pp. 14–19; Singleton, *Scrapheap*, p. 17; A. Bullen, *The Lancashire Weavers' Union* (Amalgamated Textile Workers' Union, 1984), pp. 57–60.

48. Robson, *Cotton Industry*, p. 13; Pollard, *British Economy*, p. 383.

49. Singleton, *Scrapheap*, ch. 2.

50. See the Company's *Annual Report for 1960*, reported in *The Guardian*, 17.1.1961.

51. Singleton, *Scrapheap*, pp. 168 & 190.

52. See the Company's *Annual Report for 1963*, reported in *The Guardian*, 24.1.1964.

53. Singleton, *Scrapheap*, ch. 8.

Conclusion

lthough cotton manufacturing may have begun in Lancashire as early as the 1560s, its growth prior to the later decades of the eighteenth century was relatively slow. However, raw cotton import figures indicate that the rate of expansion quickened appreciably from the early eighteenth century. By this time, too, as parish register entries reveal, numerous localities within east and central parts of the county had already become heavily dependent on domestic textile production. In other words, structural change in the economy of the Lancashire textile districts, with a switch from agriculture to manufacturing activity, was well advanced long before the cotton industry began its spectacular rise in the 1780s.

From the late eighteenth century to the outbreak of World War I, the industry expanded enormously. All-cotton cloths became its main product and it was transformed into a factory-based activity, though at a relatively slow pace in the weaving section. It also became mainly located in urban rather than rural areas and became even more strongly localised in Lancashire than elsewhere. Additionally, the United States came to supply the bulk of its raw material needs, whilst, faced with growing competition from European and American cotton producers, overseas sales to more distant markets, especially in Asia, grew to prominence. The industry became dominated by specialist producers, with a tendency for spinners to concentrate in the southern part of the textile district and weavers in the northern. Most firms remained small- or medium-sized concerns, but, once joint-stock financing was introduced in the industry during the 1860s, large-scale producers became more common. Both employers' associations and trade unions emerged on a permanent basis, their mutual interests being served by the development of standard wage lists.

Whilst the rate at which the industry grew slowed down during the later decades of the nineteenth century, its output did not begin to fall before the outbreak of World War I. Thereafter, an inexorable decline set in, albeit at a varying rate and over a protracted period. Essentially, Lancashire's cotton producers lost their comparative advantage to overseas competitors, at first Japan and then, after World War II, the Indian sub-continent, Hong Kong and China. As a result, both overseas and home markets were lost, particularly in lower-quality goods.

Whether more could have been done to counteract this decline is doubtful. Greater investment in up-to-date machinery might have helped, but, as overseas competition intensified, there was diminishing confidence amongst cotton firms that this would be worthwhile. And whilst both sides of the industry castigated central government for failing to impose adequate import controls, any benefits that may have resulted from restrained imports were likely to have been outweighted by the drawbacks. Not least amongst these were the relatively high prices that domestic customers would have had to pay for cotton goods. However, those employed in the industry scarcely found such argument compelling. After all, they faced a continuing threat of job losses and the anxiety that other employment would be difficult to obtain.

Perhaps in blaming central government for their plight, those in the cotton industry were seeking a convenient scapegoat. Yet it is by no means apparent that they were motivated by misplaced sentimentality for the loss of an industry on which so many local families had long depended.

Index